PREPARE THE WAY!

PREPARE THE WAY!

A biblical exploration of four key advent themes: the Patriarchs, the Prophets, John the Baptist and Mary (the mother of Jesus) and how these themes prepare the way for the coming of Jesus.

Alex Jacob

Glory to Glory Publications

First published in Great Britain by
Glory to Glory Publications
an imprint of
Buy Research Ltd

Glory to Glory Publications
PO Box 212 SAFFRON WALDEN CB10 2UU

www.glorytoglory.co.uk

ISBN 978 0 9926674 2 9

Printed in Great Britain by
Imprint Digital, Exeter

Contents

Dedication

I dedicate this book to the memory of Mike Kennedy, a loyal friend and inspirational member of the church.

Mike Kennedy 1974 – 2014

Acknowledgments

Prepare the Way! is my third book and, as with all my writing projects, I realise my indebtedness to many people who have helped shape my thinking, writing, understanding and teaching over the years of ministry. I would once again like to thank my colleagues at CMJ (The Church's Ministry among Jewish People), members and friends at Linton URC, and Peter Sammons (from Glory to Glory Publications) for their kindness, insight and encouragement.

This book was written during a sabbatical period and I realise that a number of colleagues took on extra responsibilities to enable me to have a significant time away from my leadership role as CEO: to you all a huge vote of thanks.

Finally, I would like to thank my immediate family, Mandy, Luke, Emily and Ben; once again your loving support has been empowering.

My heart and mind I give to You, Lord,
eagerly and entirely.

FOREWORD

Even in Christian tradition, the pendulum goes on swinging. Cranmer's Book of Common Prayer sees the Season of Advent unequivocally as an anticipation of Christ's Second Coming. Today in the West, Advent has been scaled back to a mere preparation for Christmas, the festival of Christ's First Coming – possibly reflecting not only our weak end-time theology but also our isolation of the Incarnation from the meta-narrative of Scripture. This is where Alex Jacob does us all a great service by swinging the pendulum: he roots Advent firmly and surely in the heritage of the Old Testament (in its Hebrew roots). He helps us see how the First Coming is all about God's Covenant relationship and the fulfilment of His promises of a Saviour. The Four Advent Candles are the impetus for reflections on the Patriarchs, the Prophets, on the one Jesus called the greatest of all the prophets – John the Baptist – and on the significance of Mary, mother of Our Lord.

I wholeheartedly commend this Advent study both to those who minister the word during this season and also to Christians who want to savour the spiritual richness of Christmas and to lay aside the shallow sentimentality and even Christlessness of the popular festival. If each Sunday in Advent is focused on what Alex Jacob lays before us, we will not have exhausted the Christmas story in our seasonal run-up to Christmas proper (as is often the case). After all, the Twelve Days of Christmas do not begin until Advent is over! We might even get into a healthy rhythm of looking one Advent at how faithfully God has fulfilled His word in the First Coming and, in the next Advent, of looking forward with confidence to the fulfilment of His word at the Second Coming (as does the Book of Common Prayer). One thing is for sure: Scripture is utterly trustworthy. The Christ who came at Christmas *will* come again. So let Alex Jacob revitalise your Advent celebrations and make Christmas even more meaningful and joyous!

Rev Dr David M Moore

INTRODUCTION

Advent candles –
Linton United Reformed Church, Christmas Day, 2013

In many churches there is a deep sense of joy and anticipation as the season of advent begins. Advent marks the period leading up to the celebration of the birth of Jesus at Christmas.[1] It is a time to read the biblical texts, which tell the story of Jesus' birth and help us reflect upon the power and mystery of His birth (incarnation). They also help illuminate the wider purposes of Jesus' ministry and the hope of His return to rule and reign.

Closely connected with the season of advent is the tradition of lighting advent candles. This is an important symbolic act for many churches, as it both helps to mark and celebrate the joyful belief that Jesus is the light of the world (see John 8:12).

On the four Sundays leading up to Christmas, a candle is lit in turn, each one representing an important step on a journey which leads to the birth of Jesus. While there are a range of different rich traditions around the lighting of these advent candles, there is general agreement that the first candle is lit to remember the ministry of the patriarchs. The second represents the ministry of the prophets. The third candle is symbolic of the ministry of John the Baptist and the fourth the ministry of Mary (the mother of Jesus). These four candles are often placed in a ring around one central candle. This central (fifth and final) candle is lit early on Christmas morning to remember and celebrate the ministry of Jesus.

Whatever one may think about the tradition of lighting the advent candles (or the wider issue of the appropriateness of the liturgical calendar), the key issue which I want to explore in this brief book is that the coming of Jesus into the world must always be understood as part of God's bigger redemptive plan. The birth of Jesus is therefore connected to the promises and past, present and future acts of God. Advent should therefore be a time for celebrating the birth of Jesus (His first coming) and a time for renewing our confidence in, and anticipation of His return (His second coming). In this context His first coming gives to us confidence as we await His second coming. In all of this waiting, celebrating and reflecting the profound sense of continuity between the Old and New Testaments is clearly seen.

We will never fully understand or appreciate the coming of Jesus without firstly seeing God's ongoing faithfulness to His covenantal purposes and to the people of Israel. The ministries of the patriarchs, the prophets, John the Baptist and Mary (the mother of Jesus) provide for us unique windows which help us see deeply into the coming of Jesus and the importance of His ministry, as well as helping us see the implications for our own discipleship. It is to these four "windows" we now turn.

Chapter One

THE PATRIARCHS

The author outside the tomb of the patriarchs in Hebron,
February, 2014

SETTING THE SCENE

In the very beginning of the biblical narrative, the text declares
the commitment of God to the world He created. At the focal
point of this creative work is the creation of human beings,
male and female made in His image (Genesis 1:27). Later on
in the biblical story the Psalmist declares the significance of
human beings within this creative order and states:

> *...what is man that you are mindful of him,*
> *the son of man that you care for him?*
> *You made him a little lower than the heavenly beings*
> *and crowned him with glory and honour.*
>
> Psalm 8:4 – 5, NIV

God is committed to humanity, so much so that when the initial relationship between God and the first humans is broken, God seeks to find them in order to restore the relationship and calls out to Adam: *"Where are you?"* (Genesis 3:9).

This seeking of God to restore that which has been broken and distorted and to find what has been lost is intertwined with humanity's own search for God, for meaning, for identity and for love. Early on in the biblical text we hear of humanity's search for God, as Genesis 4:26 states: *"... At that time men began to call on the name of the Lord."*

I suggest it is this dual process of God's seeking humanity and humanity's seeking God which provides the prime context of the wider biblical narrative. It is the unfolding of this epic search which takes us through over two thousand years of biblical events, eventually leading to the ministry of Jesus. Jesus Himself sums up the purpose of His ministry with these words: *"For the Son of Man[2] came to seek and to save what was lost"* (Luke 19:10).

MEETING THE PATRIARCHS

As the first advent candle is lit the church community remembers that God's commitment to His creation, to human beings and to seeking and saving what is lost, leads firstly to the patriarchs. The term patriarch simply means father (or ruler/leader) of a family (or tribal group).

In biblical theology, the term *patriarchs* normally refers to the three fathers of the Jewish people – Abraham, Isaac and Jacob. These three fathers along with the matriarchs Sarah, Rebecca, Rachel and Leah are acknowledged as the ancestors of all Jewish people. The patriarchs mark the beginning of Israel's journey. A good example of the importance of the patriarchs in relation to Jewish identity is that the principal prayer of Rabbinical Judaism (the Amidah/18 benedictions) begins with the Avot (Father's) prayer. This benediction is a commemoration and celebration that God has revealed Himself through the patriarchs as the God of Abraham, Isaac and Jacob.

It is significant in God's commitment to people that God chooses to reveal Himself and His saving purposes through a series of relationships, relationships primarily rooted in the patriarchs and linked to the establishing and out-working of covenants. God is not primarily known in the biblical text by an action, attribute or place (in contrast to many pagan deities) but rather by covenantal relationships. God is the God of Abraham, Isaac and Jacob, the God of the people of Israel. God chooses to identify Himself through relationships rooted in history. To the bewilderment of many people, God's self-revelation is not in an abstract realm of ideas, philosophical propositions or values, but rather in history through His relationships and primarily through the patriarchs. God is revealed as the God of Abraham, Isaac and Jacob (Exodus 3:6 and Matthew 22:32).

In the Genesis accounts of the patriarchs, there is a clear sense that Abraham is the founder of the people of Israel and in this context there is an exclusive Jewish motif. However, there is also an understanding that the call and blessing of Abraham is for a wider benefit: there is an inclusive goal, namely the blessing of all the peoples on earth:

> *"I will bless those who bless you,*
> *and whoever curses you I will curse;*
> *and all peoples on earth*
> *will be blessed through you."*
>
> Genesis 12:3, NIV

TURNING TO THE TEXT – MEETING ABRAHAM

GENESIS 12

In Genesis chapter 12, God calls to Abram (later to be known as Abraham). Genesis chapter 12 marks a new segment in the biblical narrative as the period of 'Patriarchal History' begins. In this segment history is shaped by the outworking of Abram's family. The text begins with Abram's call with a focus on covenant, faith and promise, and then moves on to the family of Isaac with a focus on the testing of faith. This is then followed by the family of Jacob. Here the text concentrates on the emergence of Israel and concludes with the family of Joseph, with the centre of attention being the life lived in exile under the rule of Egypt.

In chapter 12, God takes the initiative. God speaks to Abram and calls him to leave and to follow. Six times within three verses God declares His intention with the words: 'I will....' This is a call for Abram to let go of the past. Abram must leave the world he knows, the established world of the post-Babel nations with their pagan deities, and embrace a new pilgrimage with the true and living God. In this sense of leaving the past and following God's call, Abram's response provides a template for all subsequent calls to follow and trust God.

In this initial call the emphasis is on God's unconditional promises, promises which centre on blessings. Abram is blessed for a purpose- so he and his descendants may be a blessing to all of humanity.

Abram begins his journey of faith. The journey is physical as he leaves Haran, a small trading town in North-West Mesopotamia/Assyria and enters Canaan, before travelling into the Negev and then, following a severe famine, is forced to enter Egypt. The route of this testing physical journey is significant for two reasons. Firstly, it prefigures the journeys of Joseph's brothers (Genesis 42) and Jacob (Genesis 46) to Egypt and the subsequent exile and exodus. Secondly, the route is the same route (yet reversed) as the one set out in the vision of the Lord's highway in Isaiah 19. In this vision there is a significant outworking of the blessing given to Abram with the promised blessing of Egypt and Assyria alongside a restored Israel.

The journey is also an inner spiritual journey as Abram leaves behind the familiar. There is the suggestion here that part of what would have been familiar for Abram (and his family) was the worship of pagan gods. Haran was known as the centre for the worship of idols, including a well-established moon cult. Abram needs to learn to know and trust the only true God. In Genesis 12, we see this developing as Abram marks his new faith by building an altar to the Lord (verse 8) and by calling upon the name of the Lord.

GENESIS 15

In Genesis 15, the call given in chapter 12 is deepened and expanded. Abram hears again from God in a vision. God promises protection to Abram (I am your shield) along with a promise of a future reward and a permanent legacy. The themes of protection and a legacy are the themes which hold together the wider patriarchal narratives. For here Abram is a nomadic and childless man. The concern to dwell securely and to build a future family is at the heart of the events which unfold around Sarai (later to be known as Sarah- Genesis 17:15), Hagar and Ishmael in Genesis 16 and 17. The question is: will Abram continue on his pilgrimage trusting in God, or will his emerging faith and hope be lost?

At the heart of this promise of reward and legacy are the realities of descendants (Genesis 12:5) and land (Genesis 15:7). God affirms these realities by ordering a sacrifice

(Genesis 15:9). A blazing torch appears and passes between the cut meats prepared for the sacrifice (Genesis 15:17). The blazing torch is a sign and a symbol of God's presence.[3] In this action God makes (cuts) a covenant with Abram. Symbolically, God alone passes between the divided sacrifices and thereby indicates that the covenant is a unilateral gift of divine favour and that God alone is its guarantor.

GENESIS 16

In Genesis 16, the outworking of God's covenantal plan seems to take the next step forward through Abram having a son (Ishmael) with his wife's maidservant Hagar. Verses 2 and 3 imply some time has passed since the promise of Genesis 15:4, and it appears that Sarai had not conceived and is anxious and impatient. Hence, the plan put forward by Sarai to ensure the birth of a male heir. This plan brings much pain, division and confusion both here and later in Genesis 21.

In this action, in which Sarai seeks to resolve the problem of her own barrenness, most commentators see her action as sinful, in as much as it shows a complete lack of trust in God's promise. Perhaps this sin has echoes with Abram's previous understanding (Genesis 15:2) that his servant Eliezer will inherit his estate, despite the promise of 12:2. While clearly there is a sense of sin taking place, there can be for many of us a level of understanding towards Sarai and Abram as perhaps they feel the need to take action in order to try and 'actualise' God's plans. This misplaced action may well have been rooted in a desire to help put into practice God's plans.

I understand that this issue raised by Sarai's and Abram's action is at the heart of many of the struggles in Christian decision making. Clearly, as Christians we need on the one hand to know when we are called to wait and trust in God and on the other when we are called to take action and to initiate effective plans. For many this tension between waiting and doing, between the contemplative and the active, is a dilemma. Maybe it is only with the benefit of hindsight and the full discernment of the Holy Spirit that we can ever fully know if God's plans have been hindered by our hasty and wrong actions or conversely by our passivity and lack of initiative and effort.

GENESIS 17

In Genesis 17, this covenant with Abram is enlarged and deepened beyond the promise of land and descendants and includes an everlasting pledge to Abram. It is here within this enlarging of the covenant that Abram's name is changed and enlarged to Abraham (Genesis 17:5). God changed the name of our father from Abram (exalted father) to Abraham (father of many) by inserting the letter Heh. This letter represents the living breath or Spirit of God. By this new name God is proclaiming that Abraham's enlarged role as the father of many nations will be fulfilled not by human actions, but only through the workings of God's Spirit.

This new name and pledge calls for a new consecration of Abraham and his descendants; the sign of this consecration is to be the blood shedding act of circumcision of every male child and male servants within Abraham's household. This blood shedding act points forward to the salvific blood shedding act of the Promised Seed (the Messiah) on the cross at Calvary. Also in this context of the deepening of the covenant with Abraham, the promise of the blessing through the birth of Isaac is given.

GENESIS 18

In Genesis 18, the text refers to the Lord's appearing to Abraham. The Lord frequently appeared to the patriarchs and others, but not in His full glory. This fullness is only seen in Jesus (John 14:9), yet these appearances (theophanies)

An icon of the three visitors based on Genesis 18,
on display at Manchester Cathedral

of the Lord in angelic or human form are a key part of the unfolding of God's revelation and point in some aspects to the incarnation in which God is fully made known and seen.

In chapter 18, the appearance of the three visitors, two of whom are later identified as angels (19:1), whilst the third is identified as the Lord (18:10) has given rise to early Trinitarian commentaries based on this text. Trinitarian interpretation is also reflected in many paintings and icons based on this event.

For Christians, Trinitarian understanding of God is not a distortion of monotheism, but rather it provides a fuller understanding of the richness of God- Father, Son and Holy Spirit. The seeds of such understanding are sown throughout the Bible and find completion in the ministry of Jesus and the outpouring of the Holy Spirit.

THE SIGNIFICANCE OF COVENANTS

The establishing of a covenant is a key biblical theme, a theme which is woven into the call and significance of the patriarchs. The making of such covenants seems to have been a regular practice in the ancient world of Mesopotamia and the surrounding areas. A covenant is best understood as a solemn binding obligation or agreement.

Within the ancient world there appears to have been three main types of covenant which would all be marked by a symbolic act or sign. Firstly, a royal covenant in which a king gives unconditionally to a loyal servant. Secondly, an agreement between a king and one of his vassal rulers; such agreements tended to be contractual in tone and conditional in practice. Thirdly, a covenant of parity, in which equals pledge mutual friendship and co-operation; examples of this type of covenant would be that made between Abraham and Abimelech (Genesis 21) and later between David and Jonathan (1 Samuel 18).

In the biblical narrative there are five main covenants. Firstly, the covenant with Noah, which concludes with the account of the flood (Genesis 6–8), Noah is affirmed as a righteous man and this covenant is made with him and his descendants and with all living things. The rabbinical understanding is that this first covenant is a universal covenant and from it flow universal laws. These universal laws of Noah may well be reflected in the guidance given to Gentile believers in Jesus, following the Council of Jerusalem (Acts 15).

This covenant with Noah is followed by the covenant with Abraham. We have already discussed this covenant with reference to Genesis 12, 15 and 17. This covenant with Abraham is often seen by both rabbinical teachers and Christian theologians as the fundamental covenant. From the Christian understanding this covenant will find fulfilment in the ministry of Jesus as Acts 3:24–25 states:

Indeed, all the prophets from Samuel on, as many as have spoken, have foretold these days. And you are heirs of the prophets and of the covenant God made with your fathers. He said to Abraham, "Through your offspring all peoples on earth will be blessed." (NIV)

This covenant is permanent and unconditional, unlike the third covenant, which is in some aspects conditional and temporary (Hebrews 8:13). It is to this third covenant that we now turn.

The third covenant is that made with Moses (often referred to as the Sinai Covenant). This covenant is rooted in the Exodus event and is initiated by God who hears the cries of the Israelites and remembers His covenant with the patriarchs (Abraham, Isaac and Jacob). At the heart of Israel's identity is a shared memory of God's character and actions. This God is a God who is faithful and remembers His covenants. It is of interest to see the contrast (Exodus 1:8) in the beginning of the Exodus narrative between God, who is the One who remembers, while the new king of Egypt[4] who is the one that does not remember (Joseph).

This sense of remembering the covenants shows how there is an ongoing connectedness through Abraham's descendants. God is not just the God of Abraham, but also of Isaac, Jacob and on beyond these patriarchs to future generations. This connectedness is the outworking of the call which flows through Abraham and Isaac and is now renewed and enlarged through Moses, as Israel grows from a family to a tribal federation and on to becoming a nation.

In this covenant with Moses, God directs His people into a holy way of living as a consequence of their covenant relationship. This way of living is given through the Torah. The Torah is spiritual (Romans 7:12) and points to righteousness (Romans 9:31). This gift of Torah is a gift of covenantal grace, it is the gift which calls and guides Israel to seek to live fully as a Kingdom of priests and as a holy nation (Exodus 19:6). It is the challenge of living out this call which inspires the prophets (see the next chapter) as they seek to instruct, rebuke and encourage the people and leaders of Israel, both in the good times and in the times of exile and suffering.

The fourth covenant is made with King David (Psalm 89:1–4). This covenant establishes a 'royal dynasty' from which Jesus Himself is descended. This Messianic line linked to King David is a key theme within the Bible- for example, Isaiah 11:1, Ezekiel 34:22–24, Romans 1:3, Revelation 5:5 and 22:16. It is also a prominent motif in Matthew's presentation of Jesus (Matthew 1:1, 1:17, 9:27 and 12:23).

The fifth covenant is known as the New Covenant. This covenant is proclaimed by the prophet Jeremiah, who states: "The time is coming, declares the Lord, when I will make a new covenant with the house of Israel and with the house of Judah" (Jeremiah 31:31). This prophecy is closely linked with the words of restoration spoken by the prophet Ezekiel, who states:

"I will sprinkle clean water on you, and you will be clean; I will cleanse you from all your impurities and from all your idols. I will give you a new heart and put a new spirit in you; I will remove from you your heart of stone and give you a heart of flesh. And I will put my Spirit in you and move you to follow my decrees and be careful to keep my laws" (Ezekiel 36:25–27, NIV).

It is important to note that this covenant is spoken of in future terms, unlike in the case of the previous four covenants where the context is that of a present inauguration.

HOW DOES THE NEW COVENANT RELATE TO THE EARLIER FOUR COVENANTS?

This New Covenant does not annul or supersede God's previous covenantal promise to Israel. It is important to note that, within the very section of Jeremiah's prophecy referring to the coming of the new, there is a clear reaffirmation of God's faithfulness to Israel, namely:

This is what the LORD says,
he who appoints the sun to shine by day,
who decrees the moon and stars to shine by night,
who stirs up the sea so that its waves roar –
the LORD Almighty is his name:
"Only if these decrees vanish from my sight,"
declares the LORD,
"will the descendants of Israel ever cease
to be a nation before me."
Jeremiah 31:35–36, NIV

The covenants are not annulled, but rather there is a progression; the New Covenant enlarges God's redemptive purposes. Something new is taking place; Jeremiah tells us that this covenant will not be like the covenant made with Moses. This difference is best understood in three main ways. Firstly, the New Covenant is eternal while elements of the covenant with Moses will fade away.[5] Secondly, the New Covenant brings into reality a new and deeper awareness of the Holy Spirit. Namely; the Torah instructions and the on-going revelation of God will be internalised (*in their minds and on their hearts*) and deepened. Thirdly, the New Covenant opens to all people the rule and reign of the Messiah. Gentiles do not have to become Jewish, but by God's grace they through faith in Jesus are born again into God's Kingdom and are grafted into God's people (Romans 11:17–24). Those who were once far off from God's covenants are brought into God's covenantal purposes through the atoning death (Ephesians 2:12–13) and glorious resurrection of Jesus and the application of His saving work through the Holy Spirit (Galatians 3:29, 4:4–7).

Many Christians today mistakenly speak of there having being only two covenants, the "Old" and the "New". Alongside this view comes the false assumption that the Old has been replaced by the New. Such a view can lead to a serious devaluing of the Old Testament Scriptures and in some cases to a growing anti-Semitic attitude and perhaps even a revisiting of the Marcion heresy[6] in modern dress. The Bible clearly teaches that there are five main covenants, and how these covenants complement and relate to each other is more complex[7] than a false and simplistic view which sees the new replacing the old.

TURNING TO THE TEXT – MEETING ISAAC

GENESIS 21

In Genesis 21 the birth of Isaac is recorded. The birth of Isaac is rooted in God's grace, as verse 1 states: *"... the Lord was gracious to Sarah."* Within this outpouring of grace, the promise to Abraham is fulfilled within the perfect timing of God (see Genesis 21:2). Yet God's gracious actions do not guarantee peace. Following the celebration which marks Isaacs's birth, Ishmael mocks[8] the birth of Isaac. This leads to conflict as Sarah tells Abraham to: *"Get rid of that slave woman and her son, for that slave woman's son will never share in the inheritance with my son Isaac"* (Genesis 21:10).

It is worth noting that Sarah, in her anger, is unable to refer to Hagar by her name and also chooses to refer to Ishmael as *"her son"* rather than *"your son"* while speaking to Abraham. Sarah was determined that Isaac will face no rivals for Abraham's blessing and subsequent inheritance within the household. The great and distressing irony of this is that it was Sarah who had suggested (Genesis 16:1–2) that God might bless Abraham through the birth of Hagar's child.

The removal of Hagar and Ishmael clearly distresses Abraham (Genesis 21:11). Ishmael is Abraham's son, the Lord had named him and Abraham had circumcised him (Genesis 17:25–26). Abraham also knew that God had promised to bless Ishmael. To send Ishmael away smacks of gross injustice, yet within this turn of events God remains faithful to Ishmael (Genesis 21:18) and God is with Ishmael as he grows up into adulthood.

Genesis 21 is understood as a key foundational passage (along with Genesis 12, 15 and 17) for Jewish and Christian commentators. The birth of Isaac and the 'removal/rejection' of Ishmael also have huge implications for Islamic theological constructs.

In Islamic theology it is Ishmael who is affirmed and celebrated as the ancestor of Mohammad and of all Arab peoples.[9] There is, in the interpretation and application of the Isaac/Ishmael narrative, a huge-fault line between Jewish-Christian understanding and the Islamic narrative. This fault-line is displayed for example in the Koran (Sura 37), where it is Ishmael, rather than Isaac, who is to be sacrificed by Abraham. Such an understanding is not reconcilable with the biblical account in Genesis 22.

When one looks at this fault-line and the on-going conflicts between the 'sons of Isaac' and the 'sons of Ishmael' it is vital to proclaim that God has a plan to restore Isaac and Ishmael. It is in and through Jesus Christ that all the promises of blessings made to the patriarchs will be confirmed. God will save the sons of Isaac and the sons of Ishmael through His only Son and many will be brought into the household of faith.

GENESIS 22

In Genesis 22, the testing of Abraham and the obedience of Isaac are recorded. Here we enter into one of the most intense and moving portions of Scripture. The offering of Isaac is full of significance for both Rabbinical Jewish and Christian theology. In Christian understanding, the offering of Isaac is seen as pointing to the later self-offering of Jesus on the cross. There are indeed many parallels between these two events.

The first parallelism is in regard to relationship. In Geneses 22:2 Abraham is told to "take your son" (Isaac). The Bible tells us that Jesus is God's son (Hebrews 1:2, Mark 1:1 and Matthew 16:16). Secondly, Isaac is identified as Abraham's only son. This identification is in the context of the promise given in Genesis 21:12. The Bible affirms that Jesus is God's only Son (John 3:16). Thirdly, Isaac is spoken of as the son who is loved by Abraham. The Bible affirms that God loves Jesus (Matthew 17:5).

The next parallelism is in regard to place. Genesis 22 identifies the place as on a mountain in the region of Moriah – an area which is identified in 2 Chronicles 3:1 (and by subsequent tradition) as the Temple Mount in Jerusalem. Jesus was crucified in Jerusalem.

The next parallelism is the fact that Isaac is to be sacrificed. The Bible records that the death of Jesus is to be understood primarily as a sacrifice, in keeping with the true meaning of the sacrifice of the Passover lamb (1 Corinthians 5:7). Further striking parallels are found within the details of the sacrifice. For example, Genesis 22:6 speaks of Abraham placing the wood for the sacrifice upon Isaac. In a similar way Jesus carries the wood (the cross) for His sacrifice. Genesis 22:7 records the central question asked by Isaac, namely: *"Where is the lamb?"* Jesus is frequently referred to as the lamb (John 1:29, Revelation 5:6–13 and 14:1–5). Genesis 22:13 records that the lamb which is used as a substitute for Isaac is caught by the head in a thicket of thorns. A crown of thorns is placed on the head of Jesus (John 19:2) as part of the mockery prior to His crucifixion.

In addition to these parallelisms, it is also of interest to speculate on the age of Isaac at the time of this event. In most Christian writing and Christian art Isaac is nearly always portrayed as a young boy, but in most Jewish art Isaac is seen as an adult. This adult image is more in keeping with the text, as Isaac climbs the mountain carrying the wood. This would be a demanding physical task, which may well imply Isaac was a strong adult in the prime of his life (perhaps even at the same age as Jesus was at his crucifixion) rather than a young boy.

Such parallelisms and associated reflections are, I suggest, faith-building and intriguing. However, perhaps the most important point to note is the two key differences between the offering of Isaac and Jesus. Firstly, Isaac did not know what was going to happen (Genesis 22:7). Jesus however clearly knew and told others on many occasions what was going to take place, yet resolutely Jesus followed the path to the cross (Luke 9:51, Matthew 16:21–28).

Secondly, in Genesis 22:11–12 an angel prevents the killing of Isaac. However, in the crucifixion of Jesus there is no angelic intervention, although we know Jesus had at His disposal the power to call upon a legion of angels. Jesus dies upon the cross and His final words are recorded in John 19:30, *"It is finished."* Paul some years later, reflecting upon the death of Jesus, states: *God made him who had no sin to be sin for us, so that in him we might become the righteousness of God* (2 Corinthians 5:21, NIV).

The offering of Jesus for sin becomes central to the message of the gospel. His death and resurrection (the two sides of the one redemptive act of God) are the core realities of Christian hope. This hope begins in God's covenantal faithfulness to the patriarchs.

The story of Isaac continues with his marriage to Rebekah (Genesis 24). Isaac inherits all from Abraham at his death (Genesis 25:5) and, following Isaacs's prayer (Genesis 25:21), Rebekah is no longer barren (this has echoes with the earlier promise given to Sarah) and gives birth to Esau and Jacob. Isaac stays in the land (Genesis 26) during a time of famine and God assures Isaac that he will continue to be blessed as was Abraham.

TURNING TO THE TEXT – MEETING JACOB

The story of Jacob begins in an unfavourable light, as Jacob tricks his older brother out of the blessing from their father Isaac. However, it is worth noting that since the blessing went with the birthright (which Esau had sold to Jacob – Genesis 25) it could be argued that actually the blessing now belonged to Jacob and Isaac was showing favouritism towards Esau? Jacob then flees to Haran, the home of his maternal uncle Laban, in order to escape the revenge of Esau (Genesis 27). On his way to Haran he encounters God powerfully in a dream (Genesis 28). Within this dream the covenantal promises given to Abraham and Isaac are passed on to Jacob. It is through Jacob that the patriarchal family eventually becomes a nation, as Jacob's twelve sons become the progenitors of the twelve tribes.

As Jacob prepares after some twenty years to return from Haran to Canaan with his accumulated wealth, he encounters a man and wrestles with him (Genesis 32:22–32). Once again Jacob is alone (this has echoes of his dream in Genesis 28:11f). This takes place near the ford over the Jabbok stream, approximately 20 miles north of the Dead Sea. It is unclear exactly who this man is, although later in the text (verse 30) Jacob recognises the man as God in an angelic form.[10] This encounter shows Jacob that it was God alone who has held and always will hold his destiny.

Jacob has "wrestled" all his life, from the womb (Genesis 25:22) onwards. He struggled with Esau and Laban. Now as Jacob prepares to enter Canaan and hopefully be reconciled with Esau, Jacob must be reconciled firstly with God. This encounter with God is so profound that Jacob is renamed Israel. Israel means the people who struggle (wrestle) with God. We see this "struggle" throughout the outworking of the covenants. This struggle is in part to do with encountering God's kindness (mercy/blessing) alongside God's sternness (judgement/severe standards). This is the very point made by Paul, as he reflects upon the election of Israel, alongside the grafting in of Gentile believers in Jesus – he writes:

Consider therefore the kindness and sternness of God: sternness to those who fell, but kindness to you, provided that you continue in his kindness. Otherwise you will be cut off (Romans 11:22, NIV).

It is also worth noting that the Greek word for sternness (apotomial) literally means cutting off or cutting out.

Jacob is reconciled to Esau (Genesis 33) and settles in Bethel, and God confirms again the new name of Israel given to Jacob, along with the blessing of the land and descendants previously given to Abraham and Isaac (Genesis 35:10–12). The final part of Jacob's story is intertwined with the final section of the Genesis text, namely the story of Jacob's youngest son, Joseph (Genesis 37f). Jacob (now sometimes known in the text as Israel) is heartbroken to hear of the 'death' of Joseph (Genesis 37:34–35), but eventually realises Joseph is not dead and goes to meet with him in Egypt. Again God reassures Jacob not to fear going to Egypt (Genesis 46:2–4) and within this reassurance reaffirms the covenant of blessing. The death of Jacob is recorded in Genesis 49, having firstly given his blessing to all his sons. Here the story comes full circle, from the starting point of Jacob's gaining deceptively his own father's blessing, to now giving his own blessing (presented in poetic form)[11] to his sons.

THE PATRIARCHS IN THE NEW TESTAMENT

The patriarchs are mentioned within the New Testament in a range of contexts. Firstly, in the genealogies of Jesus, these are recorded in Matthew 1:1–16 and Luke 3:23–38 and in the following birth narratives. These texts are especially prominent in the period of advent.

Matthew begins his Gospel account with the genealogy of Jesus, beginning with Abraham (Matthew 1:2) and continuing forward via Isaac and Jacob up until the birth of Jesus. Matthew's account is structured in a very precise and stylised way, with three sets of fourteen generations. This prominent focus at the very beginning of the genealogy upon the three patriarchs probably helped Matthew as he wrote to a largely Jewish community, in order to show the essential link between Jesus and Jewish history and covenantal identity. In Luke's account, which is placed later in the narrative, the genealogy works backwards, beginning with Joseph and going right back beyond patriarchal history to Adam. This approach was probably important for Luke, who is writing for a more mixed community, in which he seeks to stress the universal scope of Jesus' ministry.

In the birth narratives the link with the patriarchs is affirmed again directly in Mary's song (Luke 1:54–55) and Zechariah's song (Luke 1:72–73) and indirectly in Matthew's account of the flight to Egypt (2:13–15), in which Matthew links God's calling of the nation out of Egypt to the life of Jesus. In this sense and in many other ways Matthew is seeking to show that the history of Israel is recapitulated in the person and ministry of Jesus.

In other Gospel narratives striking references to the patriarchs appear in Jesus' teaching about marriage and the resurrection. For example, Matthew 22:32 states: *"I am the God of Abraham, the God of Isaac, and the God of Jacob."*

Also in John 8, the validity of Jesus' testimony is linked with a correct understanding of what it truly means to be the children of Abraham.

In the book of Acts, the covenant promise to Abraham is an important feature in Peter's speech (Acts 3:25), in Stephen's speech to the Sanhedrin (Acts 7) and in the wider missionary preaching of Paul (Acts 13:17, 13:26, 22:14, 24:14 and 26:6).

In the rest of the New Testament there are many other references to the patriarchs in which a sense of continuity and on-going covenantal faithfulness is proclaimed. Also within these references a context for explaining and proclaiming the gospel is provided (for example, Romans 3–4, Romans 9:4, 11:1, Galatians 3:6–9, Galatians 3:29, Galatians 4:21–31, Hebrews 2:16, Hebrews 6:13–15, James 2:21–23 and 1 Peter 3:6).

At the heart of the New Testament teaching relating to the patriarchs are two complementary truths. Firstly, God's faithfulness to His promises and His people and secondly, the widening and enlarging of the significance of the blessings given to the patriarchs. For example, Paul makes it clear that Abraham is the father of all who believe (Romans 4:16 and Galatians 3:7) and the purpose of all the eight blessings given to Israel (Romans 9:3– 5) which include the patriarchs, is to prepare the way for the coming of Jesus Christ (Messiah).

It is through the ministry of Jesus that all people can enter fully into a new covenantal relationship with God. It is through the ministry of Jesus that all the promises made to the patriarchs are confirmed (Romans 15:8) and special mention within this is given to non-Jews (Gentiles) praising God in response to their experience of God's call and God's mercy.

This widening and enlarging of the blessings given to the patriarchs is seen as a fulfilment of the original promise to Abram in Genesis 12:3: *"... all peoples on earth will be blessed through you."* This promise is traced through the line of Isaac. Isaac is the child of blessing in both Rabbinical Jewish and Christian teaching.

In Paul, for example, Isaac is seen as a key to unlocking God's sovereign plan (Romans 9:6–10). Paul presents here the understanding that the election of Israel was never meant to be limited to physical descent, but rather election is rooted in Israel's responses to God's promise and mercy. From this understanding the covenantal promises are not the same as natural descent, but rather a redefining of Israel is taking place, through a correct focus on the promise of Isaac within the context of God's wider election and supremely through the life and ministry of Jesus, Jesus who is and always will be: *"a light for revelation to the Gentiles and for glory to your people Israel"* (Luke 2:32).

In engaging with the patriarchs and the related issue of the covenants, it is clear that the patriarchs despite their flaws were people of faith, people who were helplessly reliant on and radically committed to God. There is much to reflect upon as the first advent candle shines out its light.

Chapter Two

THE PROPHETS

A statue in Jaffa, commemorating the
ministry of the prophet Jonah

THE MINISTRY OF THE PROPHETS

As the second advent candle is lit attention is turned to the
ministry of the biblical prophets. In this section the focus
will be mainly on the prophecies relating to the coming
and subsequent ministry of the Messiah. These messianic
prophecies are a key theme within the prophetic books of
the Old Testament. I also want to conclude with a brief
reflection on the role of prophecy in the emerging early
church community.

Christians have always believed that God the Holy Spirit spoke by the prophets. This understanding is rooted clearly in the New Testament, for example Hebrews 1:1–2 (NIV) states: *In the past God spoke to our forefathers through the prophets at many times and in various ways, but in these last days he has spoken to us by his Son, whom he appointed heir of all things, and through whom he made the universe.* A similar statement is made in the Nicene Creed which arose from the deliberations of the first ecumenical council of Nicaea in 325.

In the New Testament period Jewish scholars applied the term 'the prophets' to a large segment of Scripture, alongside the books of the Law (Torah) and the Writings. Often distinction was made between the early or former prophets contained in such books as Joshua, Judges and 1 and 2 Samuel and the later prophets such as Isaiah, Micah, and Ezekiel. However, often the understanding of a prophet could be used more widely, as in the case of the ministry of Moses. It is in these prophets of the Old Testament that the vast majority of prophetic passages concerning the ministry of the Messiah occur.

The prophets are understood to be God's mouthpiece in two main ways – forthtelling and foretelling. Firstly, the prophets speak into their own contexts, with messages primarily of instruction, warning, rebuke and encouragement in regards to how the people should live out the implications of God's gift and call as a kingdom of priests and as a holy nation.

This type of prophetic utterances is found throughout the vast sweep of the prophetic books of the Bible. Let us pinpoint three good examples of this: firstly, in the book of Habakkuk, secondly, the book of Micah and thirdly in the book of Amos.

The prophet Habakkuk is writing probably at the beginning of King Jehoiakim's reign (609 – 598) and Habakkuk sees the forthcoming invasion of the Babylonian forces. In fact probably like the prophet Jeremiah, Habakkuk lived to see the fall of Jerusalem to the forces of Babylon in 597. Yet within his view of a horrific unfolding judgement, Habakkuk proclaims his steadfast trust in the Sovereign Lord (Habakkuk 3:16–19).

The prophet Micah is writing in the reigns of three Judean Kings (Jotham, Ahaz and Hezekiah) and sees the social and religious ills of his time with great clarity. Micah predicts the fall of Samaria and the subsequent fall of Judah. He calls for God's people to act with justice, to love mercy and to walk with humility, in their covenantal relationship with God (Micah 6:8). His prophecies have a complex mix of doom and hope.

The prophet Amos is writing during the reigns of Uzziah and Jeroboam (793–753) and challenges Israel for her corruption, complacency, pride and spiritual indifference. Amos sees that true spiritual life must be shown in genuine acts of social justice (Amos 5:24). Without this commitment to justice and true piety, God's severe judgement will come. Amos sees profoundly into God's sovereign works, as God is not simply the God of Israel, but He also has sovereignty over all nations. The destiny of all nations is in 'God's hands'. This truth is developed further, for example, in the prophecies of Daniel, Nahum and Jonah.

Secondly, the prophets speak well beyond their own immediate contexts and provide a 'window into the future', namely they share a vision or an understanding of God's future sovereign acts. Some of these future prophecies are of a conditional nature, while others appear unconditional. Also some of the "future prophecies" are intertwined with prophecies speaking into the current context of the prophet. Any interpreter of biblical prophecy therefore needs to handle and apply such prophetic texts with care.[12]

The Christian understanding is that many of these prophecies have been fulfilled in the ministry of Jesus, but some other prophecies still await fulfilment as they point to a time still in the future. This future is often linked to the return and reign of Jesus. It is to these two complementary aspects of Messianic prophecy that our attention rightly turns during the period of advent.

MESSIANIC PROPHECIES

These Messianic prophecies can be divided helpfully into four main categories. The first category is to do with the Messiah's ancestry and birth, the second with His ministry, the third with His death and the fourth with His resurrection, return and reign.

ANCESTRY AND BIRTH

In terms of the Messiah's ancestry and birth, a good place to begin is in the prophecy of Isaiah. In Isaiah 7:14 the prophet states: *"Therefore, the Lord himself will give you a sign: The virgin will be with child and will give birth to a son, and will call him Immanuel."* This prophecy becomes a foundational text in both Matthew (Matthew 1:23) where the quotation is given in full, and in Luke's (Luke 1:27) birth narratives.

In addition to the unique surroundings of a virgin birth, the prophet Micah (5:2) speaks of the Messiah's birthplace and within the same verse speaks of the Messiah's pre-existence, with the phrase: " *....whose origins are from of old, from ancient times."* This sense of the Messiah's pre-existence[13] is also spoken of in Isaiah 9:7 and Psalm 110:1. Jesus Himself spoke of this when He said: *"....before Abraham was born, I am!"* (John 8:58).

This pre-existence of the Messiah is linked to the deity of Jesus. The Gospels of Mark and John (both of which begin without a birth narrative) each commence their narrative with explicit declarations of Jesus' deity (John 1:1, Mark 1:1).

Another interesting prophetic link with the birth of Messiah is the statement made by Abraham (see chapter 1) that God will provide for Himself the lamb for a burnt offering. John the Baptist identifies Jesus as the Lamb of God (John 1:29) and in Luke's birth narrative (Luke 2:15) it is the local shepherds who are the first on the scene to celebrate the birth. There is a strong tradition that these local[14] shepherds would have worked for the Jerusalem Temple authorities, caring for the lambs which would be used for the annual Passover sacrifices. If this is the case, how wonderfully appropriate that these shepherds were the first to welcome God's Passover lamb, "Jesus" into the world. This Passover lamb theme is developed further in key New Testament texts, such as 1 Corinthians 5:7, 1 Peter 1:19 and Revelation 5:12.

MINISTRY OF THE MESSIAH

A good starting point for this category of prophecy is with the prophet Isaiah. Isaiah 61:1–2 is in many ways a messianic manifesto and Jesus in the synagogue in Nazareth (Luke 4:16–21) applies these prophetic words directly to Himself and His ministry. Throughout His ministry Jesus was led by the Spirit and all aspects of His ministry (preaching, teaching, healing, deliverance, etc.) fulfil and display the true messianic hopes which had built up in Jewish thought over the centuries.

By the first century, Jewish leaders had drawn up a list of acts the Messiah would perform in order to prove His true identity. This is probably the context behind the meeting Jesus had with the Sadducees and Pharisees, recorded in Matthew 16:1–4. This list builds on the messianic prophecies in the book of Isaiah, where the Messiah will enable the blind to see, the lame to walk, the deaf to hear and the lepers to be cleansed (Isaiah 29:18, 35:5–6 and 61:1–2). Often when Jesus carried out an act which could be understood as a messianic sign, He immediately instructed the person blessed by the act to report their experience directly and immediately to the priests, as a testimony to them (Matthew 8:4).

MESSIAH'S DEATH

The events leading up to and surrounding Jesus' death are clearly recorded by the prophets. Firstly, His triumphant entry into Jerusalem, which is recorded in all four Gospel accounts, is spoken of in Zechariah 9:9. Secondly, His betrayal by a friend (Psalm 41:9, John 18:2). Thirdly, His suffering as an offering for sin (Isaiah 53, John 1:29, Ephesians 1:7, 1 Peter 2:24–25, 1 John 2:2 and: 12). Specifically within this suffering: His crucifixion alongside thieves (Isaiah 53:12, Matthew 27:44), the piercing of His hands and feet (Psalm 22:16, John 20:27), the dividing of His clothes (Psalm 22:18, Matthew 27:35), the offering of wine and gall (Psalm 69:21, Matthew 27:34 and John 19:28–30), the fact that not one of Jesus' bones were broken during the crucifixion (Numbers 9:12 and Exodus 12:46, John 19:31–36)and the ultimate sense of having been forsaken by God (Psalm 22:1, Matthew 27:46).

In this experience of forsakenness, Jesus identifies both with the internal exile His people are suffering at the hands of pagan rulers (for the cross of Roman crucifixion was the bitterest symbol of this on-going exile) and He identifies with sin itself as He is separated from His father and becomes sin for the sake of sinners (2 Corinthians 5:21). In and through His suffering and sacrificial death, Jesus offers Himself as the perfect once-for-all sin offering and brings into reality the New Covenant prophesied in Jeremiah 31. It is remarkable and faith-building to see how the specific details around the Messiah's death are prophesied or described in such accurate and complete ways many hundreds[15] of years before the horrific events of his betrayal, arrest and crucifixion took place.

Jesus is buried in a rich man's tomb (Isaiah 53:9, John

19:38–42), due to the intervention of Joseph of Arimathea who- along with Nicodemus (see John 3:1–21), was a secret disciple of Jesus. This intervention prevented Jesus' body from being thrown out to the waste grounds beyond the city walls of Jerusalem, to be consumed by dogs and other wild animals. This would have been the normal fate for the bodies of all crucified criminals.

MESSIAH'S RESURRECTION, RETURN AND REIGN

The psalmist (Psalm 16:10) and the prophet Isaiah (Isaiah 25:8) point to the resurrection, as the power of sin and death will not be able to hold the Messiah. Jesus the risen and ascended Lord offers now the way of salvation to all who call upon Him (Joel 2:32, Romans 10:9–13). In the fullness of God's timing Jesus will return (Acts 1:11). His return will be physical, visible, dramatic and definitive. It will usher in the Messiah's reign (Daniel 7:14, Zechariah 14, Isaiah 60:19, 1 Corinthians 15:24–28, 1 Peter 5:4, Revelation 21:1–4).

The mission of the church today in sharing the good news of Jesus and in seeking to be a living sign of the Kingdom will find its ultimate goal not through revival or renewal (although these things are indeed precious in God's sight) but in the Lord's return, as Titus 2:13 states: *"...we wait for the blessed hope—the glorious appearing of our great God and Saviour, Jesus Christ, who gave Himself for us to redeem us from all wickedness and to purify for Himself a people that are His very own, eager to do what is good."* The ultimate prayer therefore of the church is the prayer of Revelation 22:20: *"Amen, Come, Lord Jesus."*

PROPHECY IN THE EARLY CHURCH COMMUNITY

Prophecy in the early church community was understood and celebrated in three main ways. Firstly, the New Testament writers point out frequently that many Old Testament prophecies find their fulfilment in the events they proclaim in the life and ministry of the Messiah. In this context the appeal to such prophetic fulfilment became a foundational part of much New Testament preaching and teaching. Examples of this are found frequently in the book of Acts. For example, they appear when Philip ministers to the Ethiopian (Acts 8:26 – 40) and when Peter declares in his ministry to the household of Cornelius that: *"All the prophets testify about him (Jesus) that everyone who believes in him receives forgiveness of sins through his name"* (Acts 10:43).

A similar use of prophecy is found in Paul's majestic teaching in Romans 9–11, where 39% of the text consists of Old Testament quotations. Paul clearly bases much of his argument about God's on-going faithfulness to Israel within God's revelation in the Old Testament. Paul emphasises God's consistency, continuity and unity in proclaiming Jesus as Messiah of Israel and Lord of all. Paul also appears to be drawing upon well-known paths of Jewish midrash in the ways he interprets and applies his textual arguments. Such an approach would have been very helpful to many Jewish members of the emerging Christian (Messianic) congregations in Rome who were well versed in rabbinical studies.

Secondly, the church knew that the ministry of prophets had been dormant in Israel for many centuries but had sprung back into life through the coming of Jesus. Jesus' ministry included His being a prophet. He was known as the prophet of Nazareth and as the prophet like Moses (Matthew 21:11, Acts 3:22 and 7:37). The church therefore taught that seeing Jesus as a prophet was part of the bigger picture of the

Messiah's calling and role. Often the church taught that the ministry of the Messiah should helpfully be understood as bringing together the three key biblical strands of prophet, priest and King. While the church proclaimed that Jesus was clearly more than a prophet, the church never saw Him as less.

Jesus as a prophet like Moses[16] brought to Israel an urgent and eschatological message. His prophetic ministry pointed to the conviction that the Torah concluded with an 'inner tension'. This inner tension arises from the promise of Deuteronomy 18:15 – namely, that a prophet like Moses will arise: but the end of Deuteronomy (Deuteronomy 34:10) states that no such prophet had yet risen in Israel. Therefore, the Torah concludes with an inner tension between Moses' literal words in Deuteronomy 18:15 and the evaluation of these words (after Moses had died) in Deuteronomy 34:10. Specifically, what Moses had promised had not happened. How can this be?

The answer is either that Moses was mistaken or that his prophetic promise would be fulfilled after the time when Deuteronomy 34 was written. In other words the Torah ends with an invitation to look into the future.[17] The Torah therefore opens the door to the coming of a future Messianic prophet. This understanding was important in the mission teaching of the church, especially among Torah observant Jewish people, as the church could proclaim that this Torah expectation and invitation was rightly fulfilled in the ministry of Jesus. This Jesus, whose life echoed many aspects of the life of Moses and whose ministry was like that of Moses, yet also even surpassed the life of Moses, for as we read in Hebrews 3:2–3 (NIV): *He was faithful to the one who appointed him, just as Moses was faithful in all God's house. Jesus has been found worthy of greater honour than Moses, just as the builder of a house has greater honour than the house itself.*

Thirdly, the church knew and experienced that prophecy

was not simply to be limited to the application of Old Testament texts to their fulfilment in Jesus or to proclaiming the prophetic ministry of Jesus, but the church also saw that the gifts of prophecy were continuing amongst the followers of Jesus as a result of the on-going outpouring of the Holy Spirit. This was in keeping with Joel's prophecy (Joel 2:28–32) which Peter quoted in his Pentecost address (Acts 2:14–36). The last phrase of the quotation: (*"and they shall prophesy"*) is not in Joel and is probably a gloss given by Peter in his address, but this gloss shows clearly that Peter and others were very much aware of the Holy Spirit moving among the early church, bringing alive the gifts of ministry, such as the gift of prophecy.

This move of the Holy Spirit was the overflow of the Spirit, which indwelt and empowered Jesus. Now the hope of the Torah that all God's people should prophesy (Numbers 11:29) appeared to be finding its fulfilment in the early church community- for in the early church prophecy could be given by women as well as men (Acts 21:9, 1 Corinthians 11:5 and Revelation 2:20), and prophecy was widely known throughout the early church, for example in Antioch (Acts 11:27 and 13:1), Rome (Romans 12:6), Corinth, and the churches in Asia Minor (Revelation 1:9).

The gift and ministry of prophecy was highly valued in the church and the prophets alongside the apostles served the church in bringing revelation, instruction and discernment. Prophecy was understood as a direct word from God. This word did not need interpretation (as is the case with a message received via the speaking in tongues), but nevertheless any direct prophetic word must be carefully tested by the church, and if deemed genuine and appropriate, carefully applied.

Prophecies in the early church community seem to have been very varied, but most seemed to focus on encouraging and teaching the church (1 Corinthians 14:3, 24 and 29), although the gift of prophecy also had at times a clear evangelistic dimension. The gift of prophecy also appears to be given freely and informally to individuals on specific occasions, while it has also been recognised as a specific ministry office within the emerging structures of church leadership (Ephesians 4:12).

Sadly as with all ministry gifts and roles the gift of prophecy can be misused. There are many possible reasons for such misuse, but the calling of the church is not to neglect gifts and ministries because of the dangers of potential or actual misuse. Rather, the church must seek the path of right use. It is beyond the scope of most advent teaching (and of this short book) to develop further the issue of the right use of spiritual gifts and the accompanying ministry structures of church communities. Nevertheless, if we are to truly celebrate the prophets, it is a work that the church must do in each generation and in each new missionary context.

In engaging with the prophets and the related issue of the prophetic ministry today, it is clear that there is much to reflect upon as the second candle shines out its light.

Chapter Three

THE MINISTRY OF
JOHN THE BAPTIST

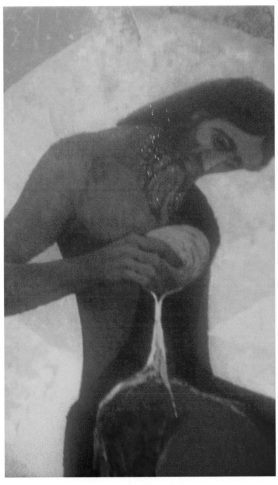

Painting of John the Baptist baptising Jesus,
by Mother Joanna from Stanbrook Abbey

"I tell you, among those born of women there is no-one greater than John; yet the one who is least in the kingdom of God is greater than he" (Luke 7:28, NIV).

As the third candle is lit the focus turns to the Gospel accounts relating to the life and ministry of John the Baptist. In terms of exploring the ministry of John the Baptist there are three main areas of significance upon which the followers of Jesus should reflect. I will begin by looking at these three areas and will conclude with some wider reflections relating to the nature of John's baptismal ministry and his possible links with the Essenes at Qumran.

FIRSTLY, JOHN THE BAPTIST IS THE KEY LINK BETWEEN THE OLD TESTAMENT AND THE NEW TESTAMENT

In trying to understand both the essential continuity and the elements of discontinuity within the revelation of the Bible, there is no better place to focus than on the life and ministry of John the Baptist. This life and ministry provide a catalyst for exploring the Scriptures with an emphasis on both the New Covenant Age (the Kingdom) which is coming into reality (through the ministry of Jesus) and God's on-going faithfulness to all His past covenantal promises.

Even a casual reader of the Gospel accounts will see clearly the important role of John the Baptist. As N.T. Wright writes: *"It is clear that Jesus regarded John as an important fixed point at the beginning of his own ministry. The early church, faced with a group of continuing Baptist disciples, would hardly have invented the connection. There is good reason to think that John himself did indeed prophesy a coming figure who would complete the work that he had begun, and that Jesus applied this to himself. Though John seems at a later stage, while in prison to have been puzzled by what Jesus was doing (and more particularly, it appears, by what he was not doing), Jesus continued to regard him as the advance guard for his own work, both as the chronological and theological starting-point for his own ministry, and as in some senses the role model for his own style, the pattern with which he would begin.*"[18]

John is introduced early in all four Gospel accounts (Matthew 3:1, Mark 1:4, Luke 1:13 and John 1:6). In Matthew, John the Baptist is introduced in the context of marking the beginning of the public ministry of Jesus. This follows Matthew's birth narratives which contain his unique Gospel material relating to the visit of the Magi, Herod's massacre of the innocents, the escape of Jesus to sanctuary in Egypt and His return (following Herod's death) to Nazareth. In Mark, John the Baptist is introduced immediately in the opening verses (Mark has no birth narratives) following the opening quotation from the prophet Isaiah. Only in Luke's Gospel is John the Baptist introduced in the context of the birth narratives as Luke records the foretelling of John's birth, Mary's visit to Elizabeth and Zechariah's song of praise. In John's Gospel, John the Baptist is introduced in the context of the 'prologue'(1:1–18), which sets the scene for understanding the purpose of Jesus' coming into the world and the mystery, glory and wonder of the incarnation, namely *The Word became flesh and made his dwelling among us...* (John 1:14a, NIV).

In terms of Luke's account, I think it is particularly important to see that John the Baptist is not simply preparing the way for Jesus with regard to making public pronouncements, but rather there is the celebrating and exploring of the link woven between Jesus and John the Baptist, which goes right back to the time of their conception and birth. It is as if the lives of John the Baptist and Jesus are woven tightly together into a shared fabric of family, ministry and message.

It is particularly moving to see how God provides practical

support for Mary as she comes to an acceptance of her role, via her extended family and specifically the example of Elizabeth's own 'surprising' pregnancy. I suggest it is the reality of Elizabeth's pregnancy which enables Mary to come confidently to the place where she can joyfully proclaim: *"I am the Lord's servant ... may it be to me as you have said"* (Luke 1:38). Such faith and trust are repeated later at the climax of the Gospel narrative when Jesus makes a similar statement while praying on the Mount of Olives: *"Father, if you are willing, take this cup from me; yet not my will, but yours be done"* (Luke 22:42, NIV).

These four different, yet complementary, introductions to John the Baptist from the four Gospel writers each affirms the sense that the Lord is doing a new thing, yet this 'newness', this move of God, this pioneering revelation, must be securely linked to the promises of the past. The new thing the Lord is doing does not cause a radical severing from the past, but rather affirms and invites many to enter into God's faithful continuity. This new move of God flows and grows from the past faithfulness of the Lord to His covenant people.

The life and ministry of John the Baptist can only be properly understood when seen in the context of the mighty acts of God which have gone before. This is why all four Gospel writers, while focusing in on the life and ministry of John the Baptist, give a number of specific quotes from Old Testament texts, while also alluding to many others- for example, Isaiah 9:7 and 40:3, Joel 2:28–32, Malachi 3:1 and 4:1–6, and Numbers 24:17.

In addition to these direct Scriptural quotes and allusions, we can see the continuity in many other ways as well. Firstly (for example), Zechariah's song (Luke 1:67–79) is full of references back to God's faithfulness: here mention is given to salvation being raised up in the house of David, the holy prophets of old and the covenantal oath given to our father

Abraham. Secondly, John the Baptist is presented as taking on the mantle of Elijah[19] and by so doing fulfilling Malachi 4:5 (Matthew 17:9–13, Mark 9:9–13 and Luke 1:17). Thirdly, John the Baptist proclaims the ministry of Jesus by drawing from Old Testament motifs such as the pre-eminence of Jesus (John 1:15) and especially Jesus as the true sacrificial Lamb of God (John 1:29). This links back to Genesis 22:8, Exodus 12:21, Isaiah 53:7 and forward to what New Testament writers such as Paul would later declare in 1 Corinthians 5:7, Peter in 1 Peter 1:19 and John in Revelation 5:12, 14:4, 19:9 and 21:23.

It is also worth noting with regard to continuity, that in terms of the ordering of the biblical books in most Bibles[20] the book of Malachi is the final book in the Old Testament. Following the book of Malachi, there was a period of about 400 years of silence with regard to biblical revelation and prophecy. Malachi is therefore regarded by most scholars as the final prophet of the Old Testament era.[21] For most people reading through the Bible, the final prophetic revelation of the Old Testament presents to them a longing for and a questioning about the coming Day of the Lord. This coming day is linked to the prophet Elijah and the promise of fathers being restored to their children.

This longing for the coming Day of the Lord is then addressed as the Gospels are read and the account of the life and ministry of John the Baptist is given. In this way the life and ministry of John the Baptist is seen as the next vital link in the chain of revelation which stretches across the silence of the 'inter-testamental' centuries (432BC–5BC) to the person and work of Jesus. This Jesus is first introduced with the prophetic voice in the wilderness (Isaiah 40:3, Mark 1:3). John the Baptist is this voice, and his is the cry which breaks the many centuries of silence.

This vital link provides the sense of continuity which

is affirmed by Jesus Himself when He refers to John the Baptist as *"the greatest man born of a woman"* (referring to the age prior to the Kingdom/gospel), but also Jesus stresses the discontinuity, namely: *".... one who is the least in the Kingdom* [referring to those who have responded to the gospel and are born again into the Kingdom by the Spirit of Jesus][22] *is greater than John the Baptist"* (see Luke 7:28, Matthew 11:11). It is important to note that this greatness refers to privilege not to stature.

SECONDLY, JOHN THE BAPTIST PREPARES THE WAY FOR THE MINISTRY OF JESUS

The immediate context of Isaiah's prophetic declaration (Isaiah 40:3–5) was the custom of improving a road or highway before it was travelled by a king. There are a number of historical records of the undertaking of such work in the Near East, as major roads were levelled, repaired and drained prior to the King's journey. John the Baptist takes this declaration and uses it as a metaphor for his ministry: he is doing all he can do to prepare the people for the arrival of the Messiah. The main focus of 'getting ready' and 'preparing the way' would be in terms of helping people to make God-inspired moral and spiritual decisions. Such decisions would then be marked by 'baptism' and accompanied by radical acts of repentance, justice and mercy.

The message of John the Baptist was a message for all the people, yet there appear to be specific groups such as tax collectors and soldiers (Luke 3:12–14) who are singled out in terms of their engagement with his teaching. Such groups of people may well have been considered by the 'religious elite' to be way beyond the scope of God's redemptive purposes. Yet such groups are not only specifically addressed in the ministry of John the Baptist, but they regularly appear at key points in the outworking of the Gospel narrative. For example, tax collectors are recorded in Matthew 9:9–13 (Mark 2:14–17/Luke 5:27–32) Luke 18:9–15 and Luke 19:1–10 and soldiers (Roman centurions) in Matthew 8:5–13 (Luke 7:1–10), Matthew 27:54 (Mark 15:39, Luke 23:47), Acts 10 and Acts 27:43. This surely reflects God's special concern to work through and among marginalised groups of people, in surprising ways.

For John the Baptist the message of Isaiah, in terms of preparing the way, also had an eschatological reality. The 'highway passage' of Isaiah 40, has connections with the 'highway passage' of Isaiah 19 which is probably set in the day of the Lord's reign, a reign marked by former enemies (Egypt, Assyria and Israel) being united in friendship, loyalty and a shared allegiance to the Lord. The preparing of the highway in Isaiah 40 is in order to prepare for the Messiah's arrival and the establishing of the Messianic Kingdom.

Crowds of people (Luke 3:7) came out to the desert regions around the river Jordan in the Judean wilderness and asked their questions in response to the message of John the Baptist, particularly: *"What shall we do?"* (Luke 3:10). This question has echoes with the vital question in Acts 2:37, where Luke records the people's response to Peter's preaching following the outpouring of the Holy Spirit. Many people responded to the call of John the Baptist and John the Baptist acquired a group of disciples.

The 'success' of the ministry of John the Baptist can be seen both by the fact that these disciples continued aspects of his ministry and kept in contact with him, even after his imprisonment by Herod (Matthew 11:2–15) and by the fact that many years later and many hundreds of miles away from the Jordan valley there was a group of disciples whose baptismal identity was found in the baptism they received from John (Acts 19:3).

Yet for John the Baptist his purpose was not to build up his own influence or his own group of disciples. Rather it was to point to and help people prepare to meet Jesus. John's ministry was a ministry of preparation and his baptism was meant to be in this sense, provisional. John the Baptist points people to Jesus, firstly by stating his own role and also by stating who he is not. John the Baptist declares, when asked by the Levites and Priests: *"I am not the Christ"* (John 1:20).

Clearly there was much Messianic expectation around John the Baptist. For example, in Luke 3:15 we read: *"The people were waiting expectantly and were all wondering in their hearts if John might possibly be the Christ."* John the Baptist responds to this expectation by pointing to and testifying about who Jesus is. This testimony reaches its climax at the 'baptism' of Jesus, where John the Baptist declares that Jesus is both the Lamb of God who takes away the sin of the world (John 1:29) and also the Son of God (John 1:34).

John the Baptist prepares the way for the ministry of Jesus by encouraging the people to get ready to receive Him as the Messiah. However, John the Baptist also prepares for the forthcoming ministry of Jesus by ministering to Jesus Himself. As stated earlier, John the Baptist does this indirectly (and unknowingly) through his conception and birth, which provides a framework for the support of Mary the mother of Jesus. However, his direct ministry to Jesus occurs through the act of baptising Him. Each of the Gospels give an account of this event (Matthew 3:13–17, Mark 1:9–11, Luke 3:21–22 and John 1:29–34), although in John's Gospel the details of the actual 'baptism' are not directly reported, emphasis is rather placed upon John's testimony regarding the identity of Jesus. In all four accounts the role of the Holy Spirit descending upon Jesus is given central focus and in three accounts, excluding John,[23] the descent of the Spirit is linked to the voice from heaven[24] declaring the love of God the Father for Jesus the Son.

It is only in Matthew's account that mention is given explicitly to John's concern about the appropriateness of his baptising Jesus. Yet Jesus reassures him using the phrase *"to fulfil all righteousness"* (Matthew 3:15). In all accounts the 'baptism' through John the Baptist marks the beginning of the public ministry of Jesus. This public ministry will be marked primarily by Jesus' Kingdom preaching, healing (including deliverance) and the calling of a group of disciples. However, in Matthew, Mark and Luke, prior to the commencement of this public ministry, Jesus faces the time of temptation in the wilderness. The wilderness for both Jesus and John the Baptist is far more than a place of retreat: it is seen as a place of significant spiritual warfare, a place of conflict and struggle. At the heart of this time of testing for Jesus is the issue of His own unique identity as God's Son (Matthew 4:3 and 4:6) was of course the very issue confirmed earlier by the voice from heaven at the baptism (Matthew 3:17, Mark 1:11, Luke 3:22).

THIRDLY, JOHN THE BAPTIST PROVIDES A MODEL FOR OUR OWN PERSONAL CHRISTIAN DISCIPLESHIP

As we explore the life and ministry of John the Baptist, we see much which inspires and directs our own discipleship. Firstly, John provides an example of commitment and courage. Throughout his prophetic ministry, his commitment and courage are clear to see, but perhaps most significantly they are seen this as he faces death courageously, following his conflict with Herod (Matthew 14:1–12 and Mark 6:14–29). Also his commitment and courage are shown in his willingness in the first place to confront the powerful ruler Herod about his relationship with Herodias. This type of relationship (Herodias was married to Herod's brother who was still alive) was forbidden by the Torah (Leviticus18:16).

It was this confrontation which led finally to the execution of John the Baptist.

Secondly, John the Baptist wrestles with doubts. For us as disciples of Jesus, it is important to realise that doubts are not the opposite of faith.[25] (The opposite of faith is unbelief which leads to a denial of Jesus). As John the Baptist's ministry is truncated by his imprisonment, he begins to question the Messianic ministry of Jesus (Luke 7:19). Some commentators suggest that this questioning does not indicate significant doubts, but rather it is better understood as John the Baptist's attempt to spur Jesus on to greater or more public ministry, which will lead to the downfall of oppressors such as Herod. I do not find this line of interpretation convincing. The most straightforward interpretation is that John the Baptist, while being a great prophet, did have doubts at times. This is quite natural to the life of faith (especially as John the Baptist languishes in Herod's prison) and maybe it is an important lesson for us to recognise and work through our doubts, rather than to suppress or deny their existence?

Thirdly, John the Baptist has an authentic lifestyle which connects with the role of his ministry. While probably very few would feel called to take on aspects of the life-style of John the Baptist, nevertheless – through the example of John the Baptist – a clear connection between ministry and life-style is displayed. Matthew 3:4 mentions firstly his clothing, namely camel hair (not fine wool) and a leather belt (not an ornate waistband). This identifies John the Baptist with the poor (also the belt probably links him to Elijah as does the hairy garment – cf 2 Kings 1:8 where the Hebrew *"a man of hair"* most probably refers to his garment rather than to his beard and long hair). Secondly, the focus is on his diet of locusts[26] and wild honey.[27] Again such foods were traditionally associated with the poor and those on the very margins of society. In this the key point is John the Baptist realising that in order to confront the powerful establishment with his message, he needs to maintain a distance from the centres of power? He chooses to live in the wilderness in his simple way, in order to be devoted to his ministry and to be able to communicate his message, without the trappings and the numerous temptations of human power and religious status. His simple and perhaps austere life-style (Luke 7:33) has resonated with aspects of Christian monasticism down through the ages. However, the key point for consideration and reflection is that whatever the specifics of our life-styles may or may not be, our faith, ministry, message and overall life-style should be intertwined. There must be authenticity in our discipleship; an authenticity which demands a holistic approach rather than a series of fragmented choices and disconnected values.

Fourthly, and perhaps most significantly, John the Baptist declares the most poignant goal for all disciples, namely *"He* [Jesus] *must become greater, I must become less"* (John 3:30). In all Christian ministries the aim should be to present and make known the person and work of Jesus. Sadly, some ministries are undermined by a personal need for affirmation, misplaced ego and selfish agendas. John the Baptist shows the need to know one's unique role and one's special calling, but always within this self-understanding there should be a central focus on Jesus. The lurking temptation for most of us is to grasp for ourselves the role and calling belonging to someone else and to seek to make ourselves central and indispensable. Jesus Himself shows the perfect understanding of and attitude towards the exercise of genuine ministry:

> *Who, being in very nature God,*
> *did not consider equality with God*
> *something to be grasped,*
> *but made himself nothing,*

taking the very nature of a servant,
being made in human likeness.
And being found in appearance as a man,
he humbled himself
and became obedient to death,
even death on a cross!

Philippians 2:6–8, NIV

SOME WIDER REFLECTION ON THE NATURE OF JOHN'S BAPTISMAL MINISTRY AND POSSIBLE LINKS WITH THE ESSENES AT QUMRAN

Firstly, what is happening in John's baptismal ministry and how does this relate to John's baptism of Jesus? The Greek word *"baptizein"* is translated as baptism (or to baptise) in most English Bible texts. The term means to dip, soak or immerse in a liquid. The purpose of this act is either to cleanse that which is immersed, or that the object immersed in the liquid will take on the qualities of the liquid, as for instance in the process of dying cloth or tanning leather. Later in Christian tradition the practice of baptism[28] in the name of the Father and of the Son and of the Holy Spirit (Matthew 28:19) was the sign (or sacrament) which pointed to a person's commitment to enter into the New Covenant community and to repent from their sin and to place their trust in Jesus as Saviour, Messiah and Lord.

In the Old Testament period baptism (immersion in water) was a key part of the many ritual purity laws (Exodus 29:4, Leviticus 15, Numbers 19:13 and Mark 7:1–4). Many special pools/ritual baths were constructed for this purpose. Ritual purity could be lost for a host of reasons and special care was needed before entering the Temple (or Tabernacle) as one needed to be ritually pure, hence the many ritual pools around the southern walls of the Temple area. It was probably these pools which provided the water for the mass baptisms which took place on the Day of Pentecost, as recorded in Acts 2.

Ritual washing could also mark a particular decision, such as a religious vow or embarking on a pilgrimage journey. From the Christian perspective, it is important to understand that the washing is not primarily in response to ethical failings (sin), it is not necessary linked to repentance, but it is linked to ritual (cultic) laws. Today many Jewish people continue with a range of ritual washing practices and the Talmud and other rabbinical writings have much material on the importance of and the carrying out of such practices. Maybe an understanding of the tradition of ritual washing sheds some light upon the practice of John the Baptist and New Testaments texts, such as John 13:6–11 and Hebrews 13:4.

Probably John the Baptist in his ministry is taking the practice of ritual washing and 're-casting' it in terms of marking an ethical/spiritual decision – the decision to mark the desire to be cleansed from sin in order to flee from God's coming judgement and to be made ready to welcome the Messiah and be restored to God's covenantal purposes . If this is the case, the baptism of John is the key stepping stone to the development of aspects of Jewish ritual practice (ritual washing for purification) to a once-and-for-all baptismal sacrament. A sacrament rooted in a sense of present election and future hope through the person and work of Jesus.

In the baptism of Jesus, clearly there is the concern of how appropriate this act of baptism was. The lurking question was framed in this way, namely if baptism is seen as a turning away or a cleansing from sin, and as Jesus is sinless, why would Jesus need to be baptised at all? The traditional Christian response to this line of questioning is to focus on the words *"to fulfil righteousness"* to signify that Jesus was identifying Himself with human sinfulness and therefore He submits freely to the act to baptism. Jesus does this in order to mark the beginning of His public ministry and to provide an example for His future followers. Also perhaps in this understanding of 'fulfilling righteousness' it is as if, in the baptism of Jesus, the whole of creation was in some sense sanctified and re-orientated to God.

This idea of the sanctification of fallen creation was developed in part by Gregory of Nazianzen[29] who, in reflecting upon the baptism of Jesus, writes: *"As Christ came up out of the waters, uplifting the whole world, he saw the heavens opened that Adam had shut for himself and for all his race."* Such traditional responses and associated reflections may well be helpful in some teaching contexts, but in understanding the Jewish ritual tradition it would also be worth exploring the idea that this 'baptism' is far better understood in the context of an act of dedication, or consecration. This act of dedication or consecration marks the beginning of Jesus' public ministry, alongside some form of ritual anointing of Jesus as the true Messiah, with an emphasis on His roles in ministry as prophet, priest and king.

With regard to this idea that baptism equals an anointing, there have been further interesting suggestions. For example, one intriguing thesis is that John the Baptist should be understood as functioning in the role of High Priest. The thesis is based on the view that the High Priestly office had been so corrupted and 'politicised' that the official office of High Priest ceased to have any true spiritual authority in the eyes of John the Baptist and others. Certainly there was corruption within Temple practices and appointments: this was especially rife in the Ptolemaic period (305BC–30BC) with the power struggles between the Oniads and the Tobiads. For example, according to Old Testament teaching, the office of High Priest should have been passed down the generations through one distinct family line. This was not the case, for during the period of 37BC until the destruction of the Temple,

Josephus names 28 different High Priests and it appears from John 11:51 that in some cases the office of High Priest was an annual appointment.

This thesis then leads to a minority view that, if proper Torah arrangements had been followed in regard to Temple practices and priestly appointments, John the Baptist would have in fact been the High Priest, following on from the death of his father, Zechariah. It is worth noting in this context, John the Baptist was also of priestly descent from the line of Aaron. Therefore, based on this line of reasoning this anointing/ baptism of Jesus by John the Baptist should really have taken place in the Temple (with John the Baptist functioning as High Priest) as a sign to all Israel of the Messianic ministry of Jesus, rather than in the 'exile' of the Judean wilderness.

Secondly, is there a link with the ministry of John the Baptist and the community of the Essenes at Qumran? The Essenes were a strict Jewish religious sect which had its origin in around 150 BC. They reacted against the corruption, as they saw it, in the priestly community, based in Jerusalem. Qumran is a remote area some 15 miles south of Jericho on the western bank of the Dead Sea. It was here that an Essene settlement was established. Their occupancy of the site was broken by a major earthquake in 31BC but they resettled the site and it grew in size until its destruction by the Roman army in 68AD. The Essene community produced the manuscripts known as the Dead Sea Scrolls, which were discovered in 1947.

Otto Betz[30] has proposed the thesis that John the Baptist grew up in the community of the Essenes at Qumran, but left in order to share his prophetic calling with a much wider audience. Betz argues that John the Baptist eventually found that the enclosed, strict and sectarian nature of the Essenes restricted the development of his universal message. It is clear from the biblical texts that John the Baptist was giving to all who came to him the opportunity to repent and to be baptised (including those traditionally excluded from religious life such as tax collectors and Roman soldiers). This sense of being able to choose implies free will, which would have been disputed by the separatist Essenes who developed a theology rooted in very narrow understandings of predestination and election.

On what does Betz present his thesis? Firstly, Betz cites the fact that the Essenes were often in the habit of adopting children into their community. This fact is affirmed by Josephus and leads to the idea that, following the death of the parents of John the Baptist, John was taken to be cared for by members of the Essene community based at Qumran.

Betz also cites the similarities between the Essenes and John the Baptist. Both are operating in the same small geographical area (the Judean wilderness) at the same time and they appear to share a theological worldview. This worldview combines a distrust of the Jerusalem Temple elite with a desire to honour the priestly with the prophetic in Scripture, alongside the practice of repentance, ritual purification and holy simplistic living. All of this worldview and practice is then wrapped up in an imminent eschatological vision drawing from the biblical prophets.

This biblical prophetic vision has a very strong emphasis on an elect group becoming a faithful remnant (the new Israel) within Israel. Also John the Baptist is seen as reminiscent of Elijah as he seeks to use Isaiah 40:3, as his 'mission statement', while the Essenes also took the very same text[31] as their call to withdraw from the wider community and set up their own separate community as an eschatological sign. Isaiah 40:3 states: *"A voice of one calling: 'In the desert prepare the way of the Lord, make straight in the wilderness a highway for our God'"*.

In regard to ritual purification there are many ritual pools found at Qumran, but there also appears to be in the Essenes' teaching[32] a strong emphasis that ritual purity must always be linked to personal repentance and holy living. In this, the parallels with the ministry and message of John the Baptist are striking. Another parallel would be that the Essenes also practised fasting and liturgical prayer and these two religious practices were particularly noteworthy in the life-styles of the disciples of John the Baptist (Mark 2:18 and Luke 11:1).

Clearly there are some striking parallels, but these certainly do not affirm convincingly an explicit connection between John the Baptist and the Essenes. Against this connection the following counter arguments can be presented: firstly, in the description of the ministry of John the Baptist given by the Roman Jewish historian Josephus there is no mention of a link with Qumran or the Essenes. Secondly, early Christian sources speak of John the Baptist growing up in and around En Kerem and there is no mention of a link with Qumran. Thirdly, there is no mention of this link in the Gospel accounts of John the Baptist. Clearly an argument from silence is not compelling, but it is worth noting. Fourthly, there is an understanding shared in some circles of Christian spirituality that the "giants" of the Bible, (such as Abraham, Moses, Elijah and here John the Baptist) are often particularly presented as strongly individualist, perhaps somewhat 'isolated' and pioneering figures and would therefore, it is argued, do not easily fit into an established and highly structured religious community, such as that of the Essenes.

The view of Shimon Gibson on this point probably best sums up my current understanding of the possible link between John the Baptist and the Essenes. Gibson argues: *"When John took up his mission and descended to the lower Jordan River region, it is most likely that he would have been fully aware of the existence of the sect of the Essenes, their teaching and the situation of their settlement. He may even have had the hope that some of the Essene community members might feel inclined to leave Qumran and join up with his movement instead. But there is absolutely no evidence that John himself was an Essene or that he had lived with them either early on in his life or as an adult."*[33]

As stated above, I find Gibson's summing up of this point very helpful, however it is worth noting that Gibson takes a different path from the one I take regarding the relationship between John the Baptist and Jesus. Gibson sees that John the Baptist expected Jesus to be one of his protégés[34] and John's questioning of Jesus (Luke 7:19) reflects, according to Gibson, John's disillusionment with Jesus, in, as much as Jesus had turned away from John's teachings and his baptismal practices and had most significantly sought to establish His own group of disciples.[35] I find no evidence for this line of reasoning or textual interpretation presented by Gibson and clearly such reasoning fails to fit in with the biblical texts.

All of the above opens up areas of interesting speculation and such speculation is often widened to include the follow up question: "What if any link did Jesus and His disciples have with the Essenes?" Again we enter the world of speculation. Clearly, if one thinks John the Baptist had a strong link with the Essenes then this would add weight to the idea that Jesus may have also had a similar link. I am aware of the suggestion that the man identified in Luke 22:10 is in fact an Essene community member[36] and therefore the Passover meal celebrated by Jesus and His immediate disciples takes place in guest rooms belonging to the Essene community in Jerusalem.

Rather than focusing in on one or two possible specific links, it is better to focus on a wider point, that the narrative of Israel (the journey from exile to restoration and the true fulfilling of Torah hope as told by the preaching of Paul and by many other followers of Jesus) is a narrative which has echoes with other 'new-covenant' movements and other Jewish eschatological sects of the Second Temple period of which the Essenes at Qumran are a prime example.[37]

SOME CONCLUDING REMARKS

It is clear that John the Baptist (and of course Jesus and His disciples) grew up and were influenced by and responded to real historical and social contexts. One can say with confidence that John the Baptist would have encountered ideas and individuals from the Temple priesthood, from the Sadducees, the Pharisees, the Zealots, Roman soldiers, members of Herod's court and the Essenes (to name but a few). His ministry must be initially understood in this immediate historical context, but his significance also goes far beyond this context. The life and ministry of John the Baptist contains a message for today, a message which helps us appreciate and reflect upon the link between the Old and New Testaments, a message which points to the centrality of Jesus and a message which ultimately can help and equip our own radical and costly journeys as disciples of Jesus.

As we have engaged with the ministry of John the Baptist, it is clear there is much to reflect upon as the third advent candle shines out its light.

Chapter Four

The Ministry of Mary
the Mother of Jesus

*A cross-cultural image of Mary and the infant Jesus, on
display at the Church of the Annunciation, Nazareth*

As the fourth advent candle is lit, attention turns to Mary (the mother of Jesus). Here we enter into the rich mysteries of God, the mysteries which surround the beauty of the incarnation and the joy of redemption. In this journey, the first question is: Who is this Mary?

In Christian art and devotional theology, Mary is presented in an immense variety of ways. Often Mary is stylised or idealised in ways which elevate her and the holy family far beyond the stark reality of the birth in Bethlehem. It is important to break free from both the distortions of extreme Mariology (the study and devotion of the person and ministry of Mary) in some Roman Catholic and Eastern Orthodox circles and the 'reactionary sidelining' of Mary which is apparent in some Protestant circles. It has been remarked that in some Protestant teaching, Mary is relegated to nothing more than a human test tube. This relegation is often in my view a reaction to extreme Mariology. In order to gain a true insight into Mary, it is important to turn to the biblical texts. We will do so by shortly turning to the main text, Luke 1:26–55, but before that it is worth reviewing briefly some of the theological developments and controversies surrounding Mary.

The first controversy is over Mary's relationship to the brothers and sisters of Jesus (Matthew 13:55). It seems clear from the reading of the biblical text that these brothers and sisters are the offspring born to Joseph and Mary (Joseph is probably dead at the time of this incident recorded in Matthew). However, this 'natural' explanation of brothers and sisters is challenged by some commentators with the suggestion that the term brothers/sisters is used loosely and can refer to cousins or that the brothers and sisters are the children of Joseph from a previous marriage. While it is impossible to rule out such interpretations, it seems to require some 'robust athletic hermeneutical manoeuvres'! Yet such manoeuvres are necessary if one is to declare the doctrine of Mary's perpetual virginity. This doctrine was taught from the late second century and became widely accepted by the mid fifth century. Alongside the development of this doctrine came the title "theotokos", which was given to Mary, at the third ecumenical council (summoned by Theodosius the second in the hope of finally settling the Nestorian controversy) of Ephesus in 431, Theotokos literally means *'bearer (mother) of God'*.

Later in the history of the church another doctrine was linked to Mary, namely her immaculate conception. This became endorsed by Roman Catholics in 1854. Mary was seen as a key "redeemer figure" in terms of reversing the role of Eve in the downfall of humanity (Genesis 3:6) and became the focus of much devotion. Such devotion often led to Mary being referred to as "the Queen of Heaven". Such devotion is often linked to the understanding of Mary's blessed assumption and is often expressed through pilgrimage. Hence the key pilgrim sites linked to Mary, at places such as Guadalupe, Medjugorje, Knock, Fatima and Lourdes.

As a result of such theological developments Mary, the faithful Jewish teenage girl, becomes soaked in theological conflict. This theological conflict has rumbled on since the early days of the Reformation and has gained new momentum with the onset of 'Christian feminist theologies'. It is argued by many of these emerging feminist theologies that Mary must be seen alongside other key women of faith (Deborah, Ruth, Esther, Mary Magdalene, Lydia, etc.) as an active faithful woman, who is an inspiration to women and serves as a true role model, rather than as a passive idealised religious icon. It is often remarked that the iconic role of passive virginal motherhood is not easy for any woman to emulate!

TURNING TO THE TEXT – LUKE 1:26 – 55

The text begins with the foretelling of the birth of Jesus. In verse 26 God sends the angel Gabriel to Mary. Gabriel had already appeared to Zechariah (1:19) and will later appear to the shepherds (2:9). It is as if God prepares the way for sending His son into the world by sending firstly the angelic messenger (both here in Luke's birth narrative and in Matthew's), whereas in Mark's Gospel the 'preparing of the way' for Jesus is the work of a human messenger, namely John the Baptist (see the previous chapter). This angel messenger is named as Gabriel (Daniel 8:16), one of only two named angels in the Old Testament. Mary faithfully questions Gabriel's pronouncement (1:34). This questioning should remind us that appropriate questioning can be a key part of faith, rather than an expression of denial or disbelief. Mary then comes to an amazing state of faithful obedience, one which echoes throughout the history of God's people, namely: *"I am the Lord's servant, may it be to me as you have said."*

The text then continues with Mary's visit to Elizabeth (1:39–45). Elizabeth was filled with the Holy Spirit (1:41) and affirmed and encouraged Mary with her exclamation: *"blessed are you among women, and blessed is the child you will bear!"* Following on from this Mary sings out her prayer of praise (often known as the Magnificat) which has similarities to the praise song of Hannah (1 Samuel 2). This song is full of celebration and declaration of God's purposes rooted in His covenantal promises:

> *"He has helped his servant Israel,*
> *remembering to be merciful to Abraham*
> *and his descendants forever,*
> *even as he said to our fathers."*
>
> Luke 1:54–55, NIV

In the light of this text (and other New Testament insights), what are we told about Mary? How should we see her? I would suggest that Mary is best understood as the first disciple of Jesus. Within her discipleship I see six important and universal principles relating to Christian discipleship.

SIX PRINCIPLES OF CHRISTIAN DISCIPLESHIP

Firstly, a disciple makes open-ended and faithful responses to God. As stated earlier, the prime example of this is found in Mary's response: *"I am the Lord's servant ... may it be to me as you have said"* (Luke 1:38). Mary's discipleship begins as she welcomes Jesus into her life. She carries Him and cares for Him. She also models faith for Him. Maybe we should not be surprised that Jesus reflects Mary's faith response as He himself faces death. Jesus knew the call of servanthood to His father's will as He prayed on the Mount of Olives: *"....yet not My will, but Yours be done"* (Luke 22:42). Like mother, like son!

Secondly, a disciple needs support. Mary does not try to make it on her own. She finds the support of Elizabeth and later becomes rooted in the community of those following Jesus. I think Mary had a unique empathy with Elizabeth. Who knows what may have become of the vulnerable teenage Mary, if she had been unable to stay with Elizabeth for the early months of her pregnancy? In our discipleship today, we need the support of others. It is wise to pray that we may find our own Elizabeths or perhaps that we may become an 'Elizabeth' for someone else?

Thirdly, a disciple invests in knowing Scripture. Clearly Mary knows Scripture. The prayer of praise she sings (Luke 1:46–55) is full of Scripture. As stated earlier, this song resembles Hannah's song (1 Samuel 2), and within her song Mary draws on Genesis 17, Micah 7 and Job. She also directly quotes from Psalm 34:2 (1:46) and Psalm 35:9 (1:47). Later

Mary shows her obedience to Scripture as she, with Joseph, takes Jesus to the Temple to fulfil the requirements of Torah (Luke 2:23). Each disciple, following Mary's example, should invest in the study of Scripture. Such creative study demands much hard work as one seeks to memorise Scripture, discuss Scripture, reflect on Scripture and above all apply Scripture to our lives of discipleship.

Fourthly, a disciple treasures what God gives. Mary treasured Jesus. She also treasured and pondered in her heart all the things said about (Luke 2:19). She displays wisdom in knowing that there is, as a disciple, a time to be open and to tell, but also a time to keep quiet, to hold on to a truth, a time to wait, reflect, refine and to treasure what has been given. It is impossible to know how and to what extent the early church was blessed by having Mary's presence and her insights. My own speculation is as follows, and based on the fact that we know that later in her life Mary was cared for by John (the writer of the fourth Gospel) in Ephesus. Clearly John's Gospel does not begin with the retelling of the birth narrative (as told by Matthew and Luke), but rather John begins by bringing out the full meaning of the incarnation: *"In the beginning was the Word, and the Word was with God, and the Word was God."* Where did John receive these insights? My suggestion is that they came from conversations with Mary – the first disciple who treasured and pondered the true meaning of Jesus throughout her life and finally shared these with John, as John sought inspiration and insight for the opening of his Gospel account.

Fifthly, a disciple does not take offence. At a number of points during the ministry of Jesus words are spoken which could be interpreted as potentially offensive to Mary, for example John 2:4 and Mark 3:33–34. However, there is no record of Mary taking offence.

Sixthly, a disciple perseveres to the end. Mary finishes

the course. From John's Gospel we are told that she is at the cross (John 19:25) when Jesus is dying an agonising death. What love, courage and perseverance Mary the first disciple displays. Later, we are told in the book of Acts that Mary is part of the community of disciples following on from Jesus' resurrection and glorious ascension (Acts 1:14). What perseverance blended with courage which begins as a young teenager, becoming a mother, fleeing into exile (Matthew 2:13), returning to Nazareth, watching over Jesus as He grows (Luke 2:52), following Him throughout His ministry, watching Him die and finally encountering His resurrection power within the emerging church community.

In conclusion, it is evident that this Mary is a wonderful woman of God, who, as a devout Jewish teenager, entered into the most incredible journey of faith – a loving mother who carried and cared for her child, who followed the Messiah and held faithfully to the vision throughout. Mary the first disciple is one from whom all other disciples of Jesus can learn so much.

In engaging with the ministry of Mary and in seeking out the implications of her ministry for our own discipleship there is clearly much to reflect upon as the fourth advent candle shines out its light.

Chapter Five

CLOSING REFLECTIONS

Wall painting inside the Garden Tomb, Jerusalem

On the first Sunday in advent only one single candle is lit. It gives out a tentative flickering light and this light points back through history to the patriarchs. Over the next three Sundays, the next three candles, which point in turn to the prophets, John the Baptist and Mary (the mother of Jesus) are lit. As this is done the light increases and the darkness withdraws, as finally the four candles together shine brightly. This reminds us symbolically that the ministry of the patriarchs, the prophets, John the Baptist and Mary (the mother of Jesus) combine together to bring God's light of revelation into the darkness of our limited understanding and our lives. Yet the light of revelation which these four candles symbolically bring is not an end in itself. The light of these four candles does indeed illuminate their own individual roles (patriarchs, prophets, John the Baptist and Mary), but the prime purpose of their light is to point to a far greater light – Jesus the light of the world. As John 1:9 (NIV) states: *The true light that gives light to every man was coming into the world.*

The fifth candle, the central candle, is then lit on Christmas morning and the celebration of His birth begins. Jesus is the light which shines in the darkness; it is His ministry which fulfils all the hopes and longings of the patriarchs, the prophets, John the Baptist and Mary (the mother of Jesus). Jesus is Immanuel (God with us), Jesus who in the words of John 1:18 (NIV) has made God known: *No-one has ever seen God, but God the One and Only, who is at the Father's side, has made him known.*

The centrality of Jesus is at the very core of Christian living and Christian theology. Without Jesus there is no gospel, no New Covenant, no forgiveness and no hope. The light of past revelation would have witnessed only to serve a false dawn and such lights would have long since been extinguished and darkness would now reign. Therefore, it is vital that in every Christian community Jesus is proclaimed and lifted high. Jesus must be at the very centre of all our worship, our lives and our message. We see this centrality of Jesus throughout the emerging witness of the early church and this 'focus on Jesus' must be the defining focus for us as church today.

In seeking to discover and maintain this 'focus on Jesus', it is however vital to see how this Jesus is part of God's big revelation plan. I suggest that you cannot speak meaningfully of Jesus as Lord without a prior deep engagement with the God of Israel. You cannot speak meaningfully of God's faithfulness without a deep appreciation of the patriarchs – you cannot speak meaningfully of God's revelation without a deep understanding of the prophets. You cannot speak meaningfully of God's redemptive plans without a deep encounter with the ministries of John the Baptist and Mary (the mother of Jesus). Above all, to know and proclaim Jesus fully and faithfully, Jesus must be placed within the wider context of His Jewish identity and the wider context of the continuity of God's faithfulness to all His promises. These promises will reach their climax in the return and reign of Jesus.

It seems to me that, sadly, this wider context is neglected or not understood in many areas of church life today. The loss of this Jewish context leads to a severing of the Jewish/ biblical roots of the faith. These roots are there to sustain the church, for as we read in Romans 11:18 (NIV): *do not boast over those branches. If you do, consider this: You do not support the root, but the root supports you.* This severing of the Jewish/ biblical roots undermines so much in the life of the church and especially makes genuine advances in cross-cultural ministry difficult to sustain (and evaluate) when there is no appreciation of the prime missionary context, namely the Jewish/biblical context.

ENCOUNTERING JESUS THE JEW

To begin to encounter Jesus the Jew we must declare and celebrate that Jesus is Jewish. We should remind ourselves that Jesus' actual Hebrew name is Yeshua. Jesus (Yeshua) was born into a Jewish family and He grew up with a great love for His family, His people, the Jewish Scriptures and Jewish festivals.

Jesus taught and showed how people could live in a right relationship with God. He lived a perfect life and fulfilled the true meaning of Torah completely. He spoke about the Kingdom as the prime focus of His teaching and the method of responding to His teaching was discipleship. Both Kingdom and discipleship are concepts which can only be fully explored and understood in a Jewish biblical context.

Whilst the ministry of Jesus brought about many wonderful new realities His ministry was always faithfully connected to the promise, prophecies and truths contained and clearly stated in the Old Testament (Tanakh).The New Testament (which is primarily a Jewish book, written largely by Jewish people about a Jewish man) presents a clear and wonderful picture of Jesus. Also within this picture there is a clear invitation for all people (Jewish and Gentile) to consider carefully His claims and His call.

In encountering Jesus the Jew, it is vital for the church to take seriously the call to prioritise Jewish evangelism (Romans 1:16) and to help and assure Jewish people that in responding to the claims and call of Jesus they are not in any sense denying their Jewish identity. What in fact could be more appropriately Jewish than becoming a disciple of Jesus, who is: *"... a light for revelation to the Gentiles and for glory to your people Israel"* (Luke 2:32).

RECONNECTING WITH THE JEWISH/BIBLICAL ROOT

In teaching about the Jewish/biblical roots it is wise to start with the essential Jewish context of the person and work of Jesus and of the early church community. From this foundation one can then reflect and apply ways in which such understanding challenges and enriches current church models of spirituality, discipleship and wider theology.

In beginning this journey of reconnection, it is important to realise that this task is not a fringe pursuit for a few interested people but rather it is a key part of the on-going renewal and reformation of the church. Indeed, the Jewish/biblical roots are an essential part of the true "DNA" of church. Without these roots, we easily lose confidence in and engagement with the Old Testament; we fail to see the on-going call of God to Jewish people (Romans 11:29). We also can lose sight of the essential historicity of the gospel; we neglect to pray for the peace of Jerusalem and for the salvation of Jewish people and above all we can become disconnected from the big picture of God's character and faithfulness.

In the past when the church has suffered severance from her true Jewish/biblical roots, the church has not simply remained rootless, but rather has sought (sometimes consciously, while at other times probably unconsciously, simply absorbing the cultural values of the time) to be connected to new (false) roots. False roots such as the root offered by Marcionism (with its explicit Replacement Theology) or Gnosticism or by buying into structural leadership values and governance styles provided by the Roman Empire, or by engaging with New Age or post-modern relativist values. Also in some areas of church history there seems to have been a link between the loss of Jewish/biblical roots and a corresponding belief in the cessation of spiritual gifts and the wider work of the Holy Spirit, alongside a growth in anti-Semitism. This certainly was the case with some extreme German Protestant groups who, in supporting the Third Reich, identified the spirit of German nationalism with the Holy Spirit.

A healthy church is a growing church. In order to grow there must be good connections with the living roots. Advent is a very good place to start to explore and foster the Jewish/biblical roots of the faith. Hopefully, each of the four candles as they point to the four advent themes of ministry (patriarchs, prophets, John the Baptist and Mary) will help all disciples of Jesus to make connections with the past, in order to celebrate the present and to look to the future with hope.

As we look to the future with hope we remember and rejoice that Jesus, the new born baby of Bethlehem, is also the light of the world, the Lamb of God and the Lion of Judah, the root of David (Revelation 5:5–6) who has triumphed and will return to rule and reign.

GLOSSARY

Adonai: Mostly translated as Lord. When stated in capital letters it serves as a substitute for the ineffable name of God (the Tetragrammaton).

Advent: A period (season) of four weeks in the church year leading up to Christmas. It also marks the beginning of the church year and traditionally is a time of reflection and preparation for both the celebration of the birth of Jesus and for the second coming. The set readings (lectionary) for advent focus upon the patriarchs, the prophets, John the Baptist and Mary (the mother of Jesus).

Amidah: The main prayer today of Rabbinical Judaism, dating back in part to the Second Temple period. There are 18 main sections (19 if you follow the tradition from Babylonian Jews of including the blessing of David) of the prayer which begins with praising God for the patriarchs.

Covenants: A solemn binding agreement from the Jewish word 'berit' meaning to cut or to bind. There are five main biblical covenants, the covenants with Noah, Abraham, Moses, David and the New Covenant.

Doceticism: A false teaching in the early church period which viewed the humanity and suffering of Jesus as apparent rather than real.

Essenes: A Jewish sect active in the Second Temple period with a main community at Qumran. This group had distinctive views about the future rule of God and strict ethical codes for living. Most scholars state that the Essenes produced the Dead Sea Scrolls.

Gnosticism: A wide ranging mystical system of belief drawing in part from Hellenistic and Pagan mythological and philosophical sources, which claimed special enlightenment and by-passed or undermined biblical revelation.

Hermeneutics: Term used to describe the method for exploring how the Bible is interpreted and applied.

Historicity: Term used to describe historical reality. Namely the degree to which something really happened as reported.

Incarnation: Term used in Christian theology to describe the process of the eternal Son of God becoming human and being born of Mary.

Kabbalistic: A mystical Jewish theosophical method of seeking to discover the true inner (secret) meaning of the Torah and the character and purposes of God. Developed in the late eleventh century, it has current connections today with aspects of New Age spirituality.

Marcionism: A false teaching in the early church period deriving from the teaching of Marcion (died AD 160) who denied the significance of the Old Testament and taught that the "Christian God" was distinct from the God of Israel.

Messianic Jews: Jewish people who believe in and follow Jesus, while maintaining and celebrating aspects of their Jewish identity.

Midrash: Term used to describe the method used by some ancient Rabbis in interpreting Scripture in order to make clear insights and teachings which would not be apparent from a simple, literal reading of the text.

Mikvah: A gathering of water or a ritual bath/pool.

Mitzvah: A command or precept of the Torah.

Passover: From the Hebrew *'Pesach'*. A biblical festival marking the liberation of the Israelites from slavery in Egypt. The last supper in which Jesus speaks of establishing the New Covenant is identified as a Passover meal.

Patriarchs: The three fathers (or leaders) of the Jewish people – Abraham, Isaac and Jacob

Qumran: The home base of the Essene community, about 15

miles south of Jericho on the western shore of the Dead Sea.

Rabbi: A Jewish religious teacher who is qualified to teach and implement the Torah and guide Jewish communities.

Rabbinical Judaism: The predominant form of Jewish religious life today which has its roots in the development of a post-biblical Judaism following the ending of the sacrificial system and the destruction of the Temple (AD 70). Rabbinical Judaism in part is a departure from biblical Judaism and Messianic Judaism as it seeks to establish a religious life with a clear focus on the Torah (without the Temple) and with a clear rejection of the Messianic claims of Jesus. There are three main forms of Rabbinical Judaism today- Reform (Liberal), Conservative and Orthodox.

Theology: Talking or thinking about God and His purposes. Theology is a disciplined and structured process where faith seeks understanding.

Theophanies: Temporary appearances of God in visible human (or angelic) form, not necessarily material. Such appearances can give helpful insight into exploring the doctrines of the incarnation and the Trinity.

Torah: Hebrew term meaning *guidance* or *instruction*, yet mostly translated as Law, also can refer to the first five books of Moses, sometimes known as the Pentateuch.

Yeshua: the Hebrew name for Jesus meaning 'the Lord saves' or 'salvation'.

ENDNOTES

[1] Issues round the date of the birth of Jesus and issues around the celebrating of Christmas etc are helpfully discussed in Peter Sammons book *The Birth of Christ,* (Glory to Glory Publications, 2006).

[2] The term 'Son of Man' is Jesus' favourite title for Himself. Jesus (and no-one else) uses the term 81 times in the Gospel accounts. The term is also a well known Messianic title and is clearly linked to Daniel's vision in Daniel 7.

[3] See also Exodus 3:2, 19:18, 1 Kings18:38 and Acts 2:3–4.

[4] This King was probably Ahmose who founded the 18th dynasty.

[5] In the context of the establishing of New Covenant living and the proportionate fading away of aspects of the covenant with Moses, there is a key question of to what extent and in what ways is obedience to the Torah significant especially for, but not exclusively to, Jewish followers of Jesus? This is a big issue in Messianic Jewish communities and within wider areas of Christian discipleship and Jewish-Christian relations. For a balanced exploration of the contemporary place of Torah within Messianic Jewish communities, I recommended as a good starting point the following two resources, *Mapping Messianic Jewish Theology – A Constructive Approach*, Richard Harvey, (Paternoster Press, 2009) and *Messianic Judaism,* Dan Cohn-Sherbok (Cassell, 2000).

[6] Marcion was excommunicated from the Church in 144. His teaching focused upon a rejection of God's covenantal promise to Israel and he understood that the God of the New Testament (the God of grace and love) is not the God of the Old Testament (the God of the Law). He rejected the authority of the Old Testament Scriptures and most of the New Testament. He accepted an edited form of Luke's Gospel and

ten of Paul's letters. His Christology was also largely Docetic.

[7] I have attempted to explore more fully this issue in my first book, *The Case for Enlargement Theology* (Glory to Glory, 2010).

[8] Most commentators see the term 'mocking' and imply that Ishmael is treating Isaac poorly, however the term can also be understand as 'playing', so perhaps there is a more positive relationship between the half-brothers? Either way, it is clear that Sarah considered Ishmael as a potential threat in regards to Isaac's position within the family and subsequent inheritance.

[9] The names of the sons of Ishmael as recorded in Genesis 25:13 – 15 are regarded as Arab names. It is argued that this gives support to the tradition within some Arab and Islamic communities that Ishmael is their ancestor. In the Middle-Ages many used the term 'Ishmaelite' in referring both to Arab peoples and followers of Islam.

[10] There are many times in the Genesis and Exodus texts (Genesis 16: 7 – 11, 21:17 – 18, 22:11 – 17, 31:11 – 13, Exodus 3:1 – 6, 14:19) where an angel appears, sometimes referred to as an Angel of the Lord. Many commentators suggest that such appearances are references to the pre-incarnate Jesus. Such reflection seems to me to be highly appropriate in a period leading up to celebrating the incarnation/birth of Jesus. We also know that Jesus taught that before Abraham was born Jesus was (John 8:58). It is also worth noting that nowhere in the Gospel texts do we have an appearance of the Angel of the Lord (although there are many references to angels), this should not surprise us if the Angel of the Lord is Jesus, because even Jesus in His humanity could not be in two places at the same time.

[11] This is the longest poetic blessing recorded in the Genesis text. Other such blessings appear in the Genesis text, for example; 9:26 – 27, 14:19 – 20, 27:27 – 29, 48:15 – 16.

[12] Hopefully the appendix in this book *"Preparing the ground-How to read a Biblical text"* will be a helpful resource in taking the next step in Biblical interpretation, application and understanding.

[13] For further reflection on the pre-existence of the Messiah reflect on the appearances of the Angel of the Lord in the Old Testament, see footnote 10 above.

[14] The shepherd's fields east of Bethlehem are only about 7 miles from Jerusalem.

[15] In the case of Psalm 22, it is generally agreed that this Psalm which describes a crucifixion was written at least 1000 years prior to the crucifixion of Jesus and probably way before any known practice of crucifixion was recorded.

[16] Jesus is indeed a prophet like Moses and many parallels between the life of Moses and Jesus can be drawn. However Jesus also reflects aspects of many of the other prophets and interesting parallels have been drawn for example between Jesus and Ezekiel, Jesus and Jeremiah and Jesus and Jonah. For a helpful exploration of this issue and the wider prophetic ministry of Jesus, see N.T Wright, *Jesus and the Victory of God,* (SPCK, 1996) especially the section on the praxis of a prophet.

[17] It is also interesting to reflect that this 'looking to the future' contained within the concluding verses of the Torah is also found in almost an identical form in the concluding verse of the prophet Malachi (Malachi 4:5).

[18] N.T. Wright, *Jesus and the Victory of God,* (SPCK, 1996 – Third impression 2001), pages 161-162.

[19] Also some New Testament commentators suggest Elijah is one of the two witnesses mentioned in Revelation 11:3.

[20] In the ordering of the Tanakh (Old Testament) in Jewish circles the final book is 2 Chronicles not Malachi. This is because Jewish sources use the threefold order of Scripture (Law/Prophets/Writings) dating from the time of Ezra, while

Christian sources use a fourfold order of Scripture dating from the earliest known Greek manuscripts of the Tanakh.

[21] Some scholars argue that the prophet Joel is slightly later.

[22] See John 3:3 – 15.

[23] In John's account it is John the Baptist who gives witness to Jesus as God's Son.

[24] The voice from heaven occurs three times within key moments in the ministry of Jesus, here in the baptism, at the transfiguration (Mark 9:7) and later as Jesus prepares for His crucifixion (John 12:28). Also the link with the voice (of the Father), the Spirit and Jesus the Son gives momentum to understanding God as trinity.

[25] I have been challenged on this point by some correspondents who feel that I underplay the seriousness of doubt and in the light of texts such as James1:6-7, it is argued that doubt should be seen as the opposite of faith. In response to this I think there are different kinds and levels of doubt and I think it is pastorally wise not to equate many expressions of doubt with the denial of genuine faith.

[26] Leviticus 11:22 mentions four types of flying insects (including Locusts) which may be treated as kosher and therefore eaten.

[27] Probably date palm honey (there are no bees in the Jordanian desert) which was plentiful from the oasis areas around Jericho.

[28] For further study on the meaning of Christian baptism see question 31 in *The Bible Student – Fifty key themes explored through the Bible, edited* by Peter Sammons, published by Glory to Glory publications, 2012.

[29] Gregory of Nazianzen was a leading theologian of the early church (Fourth Century) and was Archbishop of Constantinople.

[30] Otto Betz, *Was John the Baptist an Essene?* Biblical Review Journal, Dec 1990.

[31] See the Essenes Manual of Discipline/community rule 8:12 – 16

[32] See the Essenes Manual of Discipline/community rule 2:24 – 25 and 3:3 – 6

[33] Shimon Gibson, *The Cave of John the Baptist,* Arrow Books, 2005, *page 149.*

[34] Shimon Gibson, *The Cave of John the Baptist, page 189.*

[35] Shimon Gibson, *The Cave of John the Baptist, page 184.*

[36] This suggestion is that this man was an Essene "monk" and only a monk would be carrying water as normally this was women's work. So it is argued the reference to a man carrying water is really a well-known code for an Essene. Also some suggest that if the Passover was at an Essene guest house, then clearly the celebration would have taken place following the Essene calendar. This calendar is slightly different from the main Jewish calendar and this fact may shed some light upon the dating of events towards the arrest and crucifixion of Jesus.

[37] For a fuller discussion of this point see N.T. Wright, *Paul and the Faithfulness of God* (part 3) published by SPCK, especially the section on 'the eschatological challenge of redefined election', pages 1128 – 1257.

BIBLIOGRAPHY

Blaiklock E.M, *Commentary on The New Testament,* Hodder and Stoughton, 1977.

Chilton Bruce, *A Galilean Rabbi and His Bible,* SPCK, 1984.

Crombie Kelvin, *In Covenant with Jesus,* Heritage Resources, 2012.

Dapaah Daniel, *The Relationship between John the Baptist and Jesus,* University Press of America, 2005.

Dunn James, *Jesus, Paul and the Gospels,* Eerdmans, 2011.

Ferguson Everett, *Baptism in the Early Church,* Eerdmans, 2009.

Fuller Reginald, *A Critical Introduction to the New Testament,* Duckworth, 1979.

Gibson Shimon, *The Cave of John the Baptist,* Arrow Books, 2005.

Jacob Alex, *The Case for Enlargement Theology,* Glory to Glory Publications, 2010.

Jacobs Louis, *Concise Companion to the Jewish Religion,* Oxford University Press, 1999.

Kidner Derek, *Genesis* (Tyndale Old Testament Commentaries), Inter-Varsity Press, 1967.

Mckelvey R.J, *Pioneer and Priest,* Pickwick Publications, 2013.

Payne, D.F, *Genesis and Exodus* (Scripture Union Bible Study Books), Scripture Union Press, 1970.

Sammons Peter, *The Birth of Christ,* Glory to Glory Publications, 2006.

Sandmel Samuel, *Judaism and Christian Beginnings,* Oxford University Press, 1978.

Scott, Julius.J, *Jewish Backgrounds of the New Testament,* Baker Books, 1995.

Soggin, Alberto.J, *Israel in the Biblical Period,* T and T Clark, 2001.

Soulen, Kendall.R, *The Divine Name(s) and the Holy Trinity* (volume 1), John Knox Press, 2011.

Taylor Joan, *The Essenes, the Scrolls and the Dead Sea,* Oxford University Press, 2012.

Torrance David. W,(Editor) *The Witness of the Jews to God,* Handsel Press, 1982.

Wright N.T, *Jesus and the Victory of God,* SPCK, 1996; *Paul and the Faithfulness of God,* SPCK, 2013.

Young Brad. H, *Jesus the Jewish Theologian,* Hendrickson Publishers, 1995.

APPENDIX

PREPARING THE GROUND –
HOW TO READ A BIBLICAL TEXT

As a Christian, I understand that the Bible is the supreme authority for what we as Christians believe and how we try to live. I understand that this authority flows from the sovereignty of God. God is sovereign not just in His engagement with humanity, but also in His revelation of Himself to humanity. The Bible is a factor and a component part in the redeeming work of God, as the Bible accurately and fully communicates God's ways and His redeeming acts. The Bible also teaches how humanity should respond in the light of God's redeeming acts. Therefore, how we read, teach, preach and apply the message of the Bible is of very great importance.

"I have sought Your face with all my heart" (Psalm 119:58) In terms of understanding any biblical text in a spiritually reflective and faithful way, I believe that there are certain steps which need to be taken by the reader/hearer. My starting point is based on the belief that the meaning of any biblical text is not hidden away in some obscure secret zone, which results in a text only being understandable by (or revealed to) a select few, who have special interpretive skills or who are part of an elect group. Such a view would have been promoted by certain Gnostic sects and by practitioners of parts of the Kabbalistic tradition today, but rather, I believe that God in His revelation through Scripture desires to make the Scriptures clear (the perspicacity of Scripture) and the truths they contain consistent to any and all sincere readers/ hearers of the text through the illumination of the Holy Spirit.
Equally God does not make the truths of His Word known

to the casual observer, or the proud self-centred student, but God does make His Word known to the humble sincere seeker. Therefore, the first step in gaining a true understanding of any biblical text is to examine our life and our motivation for gaining understanding and to try and develop a sincere heartfelt desire to gain godly understanding.

"May my cry come before You O Lord; give me understanding according to Your word" (Psalm 119:169)

The second step which flows from the first, is to set time and space aside to read the text carefully and prayerfully. As we mull the text over in our minds, we ask for God's help in engaging with and understanding the text. A prayer along the lines of the following can be helpful: *"Lord help me to understand Your word, set me free from a false worldview or rash insights but rather renew my mind and deepen my capacity to receive Your truth by the gentle work of Your Holy Spirit."*

"Do your best to present yourself to God as one approved, a workman who does not need to be ashamed and who correctly handles the word of truth" (2 Timothy 2:15).

The third step is to invest time in studying the text. A good study of a text begins with assessing the grammatical, historical and textual context of a text. A text should be interpreted initially by its most plain meaning. Words should be interpreted consistently in the same context. A word can have a number of meanings, but only one true meaning in each case in terms of the author's intent. Also the first time a word or idea is introduced it will bring with it certain information which should help to guide in regards to the future understanding of other usage (principle of first use) of the word. Equally, a text may have many useful applications, but I think it can only have one central meaning based on the author's intent. In this initial step of study one should also take into account literary genres, symbolism (figurative and non-figurative symbolism) and figures of speech. Also in recognising prophetic texts, one must see that a prophecy can have an immediate historical context, a later historical context, or even a yet to be fulfilled future context. Also prophecies may be conditional or unconditional, specific or general in their application.

From this good beginning within the area of study, it is important to go on to explore historical questions based upon the text. For example, who is the author, when was it written, to whom was it written and for what purpose? In attempting to answer these questions we need to draw on the insights of various commentators, theologians and scholars. As we weigh up their insights it seems to me that one can place such insights and ideas on a scale which ranges from the impossible, to the possible, on to the probable and ending with the definite. Also we begin to see how a particular idea or theme fits in with other biblical texts (the principle of correlation) written by the same author and then on to texts from other sources. In this way, I believe one sees how Scripture interprets, clarifies and affirms Scripture.

"When you come together, everyone has a hymn or a word of instruction, a revelation, a tongue or an interpretation. All of these must be done for the strengthening of the church" (1 Corinthians 14:26).

The fourth step is to share and discuss the fruits of our study with others. I believe group Bible studies are very important as we learn from and challenge each other's interpretation and understanding. It is often only in as group context that we discover the complexity of a text, or perhaps the different layers of understanding within a text. I think it is especially helpful when such study groups are made up of Christians who have different backgrounds, or come from different church traditions and who also have a range of life experiences. We learn as we listen and engage with each other. We make space to discern the authenticity of the Holy Spirit's work in and through each other. We also recognise and value those amongst us who have particular teaching gifts within the church and who reflect Christ-like pastoral wisdom.

"Do not merely listen to the word, and so deceive yourselves. Do what it says" (James 1:22).
The fifth step is to apply the text to our lives. Study in not meant to be an end in itself, but rather we study in order to revere God, to worship and to serve obediently and effectively. Sometimes the application of a text is very straightforward. It may not be easy to apply, but nevertheless it is clear. At other times with other texts it is not clear how we apply such understanding, but we store away our insight. Maybe in the future the application of that insight may become clear or the understanding from that text may help in interpreting and applying other texts.

"The Spirit searches all things, even the deep things of God" (1 Corinthians 2:10).
The sixth and final step is to reflect upon how we (and others) have applied a textual understanding. Maybe with experience and the promptings of the Spirit, we feel the text has been misunderstood in some way or perhaps misused or even abused. Maybe a new historical, cultural or personal context means that we seek to apply the text in a different way? As we reflect upon these six steps, we also know that we never come to the end of learning from and engaging with a biblical text.

The full truth of God can never be fully pinned down. No method of biblical study can fully capture the grandeur of the Lord and His ways. The Lord always has more light to give to us, and to bring to His revealed Word. Therefore, the six steps of interpretation do not take us on a linear journey to a single goal of personal insight, but rather along a deepening circle of lifelong study and committed discipleship. Discipleship enriched by being part of a Christian community and inspired and empowered by the powerful prompting and gentle calling of the Holy Spirit.

More books from Glory to Glory Publications:

Ready or Not – He is Coming Stephanie Cottam
The Bible speaks of Jesus as the Bridegroom, and His followers as His Bride. The Day of His return for her will be a glorious day of rejoicing – but what exactly does all of this mean? What can we learn from the traditional Jewish wedding customs about "that glorious Day"? What does the relationship between a Jewish Bride and her groom tell us of our relationship with our Saviour, Jesus? And what does it mean for the Bride to have "prepared herself"? In *Ready or Not – He is Coming* Stephanie Cottam explores the biblical marriage rites in the light of Christian revelation and brings Jesus' simile to life in a straightforward and disarmingly simple way, but with a stark warning: Jesus was crystal clear that when He returns, not everyone will be ready for Him. Some will make their excuses and decline His invitation. Some of His watchmen will be asleep, spiritually speaking. A high proportion of foolish maidens will have no oil in their lamps – both groups will be left outside the wedding feast. What sort of a follower of Jesus are you? Are you prepared and ready – or half asleep, seeking other diversions during His long absence?

The Birth of Christ Peter Sammons
This book makes a powerful and compelling case for the authenticity and truth of the accounts in the birth narratives of the New Testament. The reader is taken through the biblical and historical background to the nativity of the Lord Jesus Christ. The significance of each aspect is explained, including the virgin conception, the visit of the magi, the flight to Egypt and many other topics. Detailed appendices provide useful guidance on many matters, including the fulfilment of particular Old Testament messianic prophecies and the complete reliability of the Scriptures.

www.glorytoglory.co.uk